Henrik Ibsen

A DOLL'S HOUSE

Henrik Ibsen

A DOLL'S HOUSE

With Introduction and Notes by

M.S. KUSHWAHA

Department of English
Lucknow University, Lucknow
India

LAXMI PUBLICATIONS (P) LTD.

INDIA • USA • GHANA • KENYA

HENRIK IBSEN 'A DOLL'S HOUSE'

Printed and bound in India
New Edition
OLD ISBN 033-392-161-6
NEW ISBN 978-93-5138-082-5

Published in India by

Laxmi Publications (P) Ltd.
113, GOLDEN HOUSE, DARYAGANJ,
NEW DELHI - 110002, INDIA
Telephone : 91-11-4353 2500, 4353 2501
Fax : 91-11-2325 2572, 4353 2528
www.laxmipublications.com
info@laxmipublications.com

Printed at : Repro Knowledgecast Limited, Thane

CONTENTS

General Introduction

I. IBSEN THE MAN

Ibsen's work is basically linked with the circumstances of his life.' ... it would be difficult to find another author,' writes Janko Lavrin, 'whose work is so closely interwoven with his own inner quest, with his personal crises and aspirations, as is the case with Ibsen.'[1] As another critic, P. F. D. Tennant, points out, 'The situation in Ibsen's own family seems to form a background upon the pattern of which the situations of his plays are constructed.'[2] Thus, for a proper understanding of Ibsen's plays, it is absolutely necessary to have some knowledge of Ibsen the man.

Henrik Johan Ibsen, to give his full name, was born on 20 March 1828, in a small shipping town, Skien, in Norway. He was the eldest of his four brothers and one sister. His father, Knud Ibsen, was a well-to-do businessman, and his early childhood, as he recalls in *Peer Gynt*, was spent in splendour and gaiety. However, his father became bankrupt when Ibsen was only eight years old. Nothing was left of their possessions except a small farm, a couple of miles north of town, where the family had to move for shelter. Neglected by their rich relations and virtually *déclassé*, the Ibsens remained here for seven or eight years in total obscurity. 'The ground was thus prepared', as John Gassner observes, 'for the future writer who was to castigate the false respectability and complacency of the middle classes.'[3]

---

[1] *Ibsen: An Approach*, p. 1.

[2] *Ibsen's Dramatic Technique*, p. 23.

[3] *Masters of the Drama*, p. 357.

Ibsen's days at the farm passed in solitary musings, reading, and drawing. For some time he attended a small private school in the town, but had to cut this short in order to earn his living. He was only sixteen when he moved to Grimstad, a tiny coastal town, to serve as an apprentice to an apothecary.

Ibsen's lot did not improve even when he entered into service. His days in Grimstad, where he lived for six years, were spent mostly in wretched poverty. He was despised by the local gentry whom he often lampooned and caricatured. It was here that he became involved with a maidservant ten years his senior, and became, at the age of eighteen, the father of an illegitimate son, Hans Jacob, whom he had to support for fourteen years. This event not only brought him down in the scale of society but also left an indelible imprint on his subsequent life. His recurring theme of guilt and retribution as well as the appearance of a fairly large number of illegitimate children in his plays may, indeed, be traced to this source. However, it was during this period that he started writing poetry, and formed a circle of callow literary youths. His prospects brightened a little after 1847. He now engaged a tutor to prepare him for matriculation. With him he read Cicero's orations against Catiline, which inspired him to write his first play, *Catilina*, in 1849. The play was published in 1850 at the expense of his friend, Ole Schulerud. Though it drew but little attention and proved a financial disappointment,[4] the play, as H. Koht points out, was historically significant:

> One would have expected the book to attract attention, for dramas of this kind were rare in the country. The new Norway, which was determined to create an independent literature, had not yet been able to foster a native drama. Although the capital had had a permanent theatre since 1827, this had subsisted chiefly on foreign plays. Of serious contemporary plays in Norwegian there existed hardly more than a dozen, and Henrik Wergeland was the only dramatist worth mentioning. Since the publication of his *The Venetians* (*Venetianerne*) in 1843, not a single new drama had appeared in print. *Catiline* was therefore an event in Norwegian literature.[5]

---

[4] Of the 250 copies of *Catilina* sent to the booksellers, 205 were left unsold.

[5] *The Life of Ibsen,* I, 50.

Ibsen gave up his position at the apothecary's, and moved to Christiania (now Oslo) in April 1850. Here he wrote his second play, *The Warrior's Barrow,* which was staged by Christiania Theatre in the autumn of 1850. The show brought him no profit except a free ticket to the theatre, but this in itself was no small gain. It gave him an opportunity of a closer view of the theatrical world. For some time he worked also as a drama critic and journalist. In November 1851 he left Christiania and joined Ole Bull's National Theatre at Bergen as 'drama critic'.

In February 1852 the management of the Bergen National Theatre granted Ibsen a stipend to facilitate his trip abroad. He was to make a study of the theatres of Denmark and Germany, and was pledged to act on his return as Stagemanager and instructor at Bergen for five years. This tour, as P. F. D. Tennant observes, 'played an important part in broadening his vision and giving him a sense of stage effect which his earlier plays and critical articles entirely ignored'.[6]

Ibsen's job at the Bergen National Theatre consisted not only in helping the production but also in writing plays for the theatre. It was here that he wrote his nationalistic plays, *St. John's Eve* (1953), *Lady Inger of Ostraät* (1855), *The Feast at Solhaug* (1856) and *Olaf Liljekrans* (1857).

Ibsen left Bergen in the autumn of 1857 to join the Norwegian Theatre at Christiania as its director. He was there for six years, but this proved a period of great stress and strain. Fortune struck him harder than ever. The theatre, which was already a shaky affair, became even more so under his management. It sank into financial difficulties until it was forced to close down in 1862. Earlier, Ibsen had suffered a great disappointment when, in 1860, his application for a travelling stipend was rejected by the government. The only happy event of this period was his marriage with Susanna Thoresen—a step-daughter of the popular authoress Magdalene Thoresen. She proved a source of strength to him during these lean years of misery and frustration.

Ibsen had to spend two years more in Christiania before he was able to leave Norway. These intervening years were the gloomiest

---

[6] *Ibsen's Dramatic Technique* p. 39.

in his life. He had to struggle along from day to day without any assured income. The publication of his first realistic drama, *Love's Comedy* (1862), brought him only disrepute. 'I was excommunicated,' he recalled in 1870, 'everyone was against me.'[7] He could breathe a sigh of relief only when he left his country on 5 April, 1864.

Ibsen's departure from Norway marks a new era both in his life and his work. Not only did the quality of his work change but his life also took a turn for the better. In fact, all his life and work falls into two dissimilar and distinct periods—the one preceding and the other following this date. The earlier period was a period of apprenticeship and struggle while the later period is a period of success and achievement. Ibsen discovered his true genius only after he had left Norway. Had he remained in his country he would probably have become a great national dramatist, but he could hardly have won the fame he enjoys today. The distance from the homeland was necessary to give him freedom and the right perspective. His dramatic art bloomed on foreign soil. However, one should not minimize the importance of the earlier period, for all his later plays are coloured and conditioned by his experiences of these years.[8] As H. Koht astutely observes, 'Life had to wound his soul till it bled before his writing could proceed from bitter need, from an inner strife which demanded dramatic expression.'[9]

Except for two short visits to Norway in 1874 and 1885, Ibsen continued to live abroad for twenty-seven years. The first five of these years were spent in Italy, and the remainder of the time mostly in Germany, first at Dresden and afterwards at Munich. It was during this period that he wrote his famous plays, beginning with *Brand* (1866), which made him the leading dramatist of the day. When Ibsen returned to Norway in 1891, he had already become a world celebrity. His last four plays—*The Master Builder* (1892), *Little Eyolf* (1894), *John Gabriel Borkman* (1896), and *When We Dead Awaken* (1899)—were written here.

---

[7] Cited, H. Koht, *The Life of Ibsen*, I, p. 199.

[8] Cf. P. F. D. Tennant, '...it seems as though Ibsen's whole career as a dramatist was conditioned by a desire to get even with a state of affairs which had made his childhood and youth such painful memories for him' (ibid., p. 26).

[9] Ibid., I, p. 81.

This later period of Ibsen's life was comparatively smooth and uneventful. With a gradual improvement in his financial position after the publication of *Brand,* he devoted himself exclusively to his art, and continued to produce one play almost every other year till his health gave way in 1900. In the spring of this year he suffered a paralytic attack from which he never recovered. After five years of gradual physical decline, he died on 23 May, 1906. His funeral was arranged by the government, and he was buried with all the solemnities that befitted a distinguished citizen. As the German critic, Alfred Kerr, ironically observed, 'the ruling men in Norway had a daemon among them, and they buried a grandee'.[10]

II. IBSEN'S DEVELOPMENT AS A DRAMATIST

Ibsen's career as a dramatist spans a period of fifty years. His first play, *Catilina,* was published in 1850, and his last play *When We Dead Awaken,* in 1899. His creative period, thus, covers the second half of the nineteenth century. During this long period, he wrote twenty-five plays, producing one play almost every alternate year.[11]

Ibsen's journey from *Catilina* to *When We Dead Awaken* is a long one. It is characterized by various phases or stages of his artistic development. These changes are clearly reflected in his plays which may roughly be divided into the following categories:

1. Nationalistic plays,
2. Poetic plays,
3. Modern, realistic, 'moralist' or problem plays, or 'the drama of ideas',
4. Psychological or 'humanistic' plays,
5. Metaphysical, spiritual, or 'visionary' plays.

The first phase of Ibsen's writing, which comprises nine plays from *Catilina* to *The Pretenders*—the ones preceding his departure from Norway, was dominated by his desire to build up a national theatre. All these plays, excepting *Catilina* and *Love's Comedy,* are based on national history, folklore, legends or sagas, and aim at

---

[10] Cited, H. Koht, II, p. 326.

[11] For full details see 'Chronological List of Ibsen's Plays', p. xxxix.

reminding the people of their glorious past. *Catilina* and *Love's Comedy* differ only in so far as they treat of Roman history and the contemporary problems respectively. The latter, in its radical treatment of love and marriage, presages Ibsen's realistic drama of the later stage. However, all these plays are traditional in form, and written in verse. As H. Koht observes, 'It is too clearly evident that Ibsen is following the fashion and demand of his times, not a demand within himself.'[12] In fact, these plays mark off Ibsen's period of apprenticeship and experiment.

Ibsen's intrinsic work as a dramatist begins only after he left Norway. As C. M. Bradbrook remarks, 'Ibsen did not become a great dramatist until he broke away from the stage.'[13] The first *fruits of* this new-found freedom were the two plays, *Brand* and *Peer Gynt,* which stand in a class by them. For want of a better name, we may call them 'poetic dramas', though we should not forget that all of Ibsen's plays are poetic in essence.[14] Like his earlier plays, they are written in verse, but unlike them, they are built on fantasy and sheer imagination. *Brand* is the story of a fanatic while *Peer Gynt* relates the tale of an audacious libertine. The plays, which were expressly not intended for the stage, are remarkable for their vigorous poetry and extravagant fancy. They are the best and strongest expressions of Ibsen's romanticism, and 'form a kind of bank for Ibsen to draw on in all his later plays'.[15]

It was, however, the third phase of Ibsen's writing which made him famous and earned him the title of the 'father of the modern drama'.[16] It was during this period, which extends from *The League of Youth* to *An Enemy of the People* that he wrote the plays that are variously described as 'social', 'realistic' or 'problem' plays. Here Ibsen turns his gaze from romanticism to the stark realities of the world around him. He takes contemporary social problems as the subjects of these plays, and submits them to a radical revaluation.

---

[12] *The life of Ibsen*, I, 65.

[13] *Ibsen the Norwegian* p. 27.

[14] H. Koht emphasizes this fact in the opening sentence of *The Life of Ibsen* (I, 1). C. M. Bradbrook, too, holds that 'the root of his greatest plays remains a poetic unity, a single vision, even when they are not written in verse' (op. cit., p. 3).

[15] Eric Bentley, *The Playwright as Thinker*, p. 91.

[16] John Gassner, *Masters of the Drama,* p. 354.

In these plays, as G. B. Shaw puts it, the 'problems of conduct and character of personal importance to the audience are raised and suggestively discussed'.[17] They are frontal attacks on the prevailing moral values and social norms. In them Ibsen appears in his celebrated role of a prophet and social reformer as represented, at its best, in Shaw's *The Quintessence of Ibsenism* (1891). The only exception is *Emperor and Galilean,* which is a historical play of philosophic import.[18]

The Wild Duck (1884) heralds the next stage of Ibsen's writing: psychological or humanistic plays. They include *Rosmersholm* (1886), *The Lady from the Sea* (1888), and *Hedda Gabbler* (1890). In these plays Ibsen turns from society to the individual, from public issues to private questions. He abandons moral for psychological motivation. In fact, these plays are the studies of the workings of the human mind. *Hedda Gabbler,* for instance, is a psychological study of a destructive woman. The change is clearly reflected in *Rosmersholm* in which an idealist loses his interest in reforming his community. Besides, the plays mark a change in Ibsen's dramatic technique. In them, for the first time, Ibsen makes a conspicuous and effective use of symbols and myths. As George Steiner puts it, 'with the toy forest and imaginary hunt of old Ekdal in *Wild Duck,* drama returns to a use of effective myth and symbolic action which had disappeared from the theatre since the late plays of Shakespeare'.[19]

The last four plays, which were written after Ibsen's return to Norway, constitute the last phase of his dramatic writing. They are, as J. Lavrin observes, 'partly tragic monographs of individual conscience, and partly transposed confessions of the author himself'.[20] Here Ibsen moves away from the realm of individual psyche to that of individual conscience. 'His concern is rather with the inner experience of the individual, with his often unaided exploration of that experience, with the reassessment and revaluation of his past at some ultimate turning-point of his soul's pilgrimage.'[21] He turns his back completely on the stage and the external world, and

---

[17] 'The Quintessence of Ibsenism', *Major Critical Essays*, p. 137.

[18] For a detailed discussion on the plays of this group, see the following section, 'Ibsen and the Social Drama.'

[19] *The Death of Tragedy,* p. 292.

[20] *Ibsen: An Approach*, p. 12.

[21] Una Ellis-Fermor, Introduction to Ibsen's *The Master Builder and Other Plays* (Penguin Books, 1958), p. 7.

focuses his attention on the inner self. The plays are, as C. M. Bradbrook rightly suggests, 'the dramatic equivalent of the self-analysis of Kierkegaard'.[22] Their central theme is the remorse of conscience, and they are, technically, more or less static. There is hardly any plot or action in the old sense. As P. F. D. Tennant points out, they take on the character of 'an armchair conversation, recalling forgotten memories, and waiting for the hand of fate to mete out its punishment in the last act'.[23]

Some critics think that these last plays show a decline in Ibsen's power. C. M. Bradbrook, for instance, holds that 'these plays are written in descending order of dramatic greatness'.[24] This view is also shared by John Gassner, who observes that 'deterioration in Ibsen's craftsmanship starts with *The Master Builder*. ...his plays become obscure or thin out, and the decline is, in the main, progressive'.[25] However, there are a few critics who take an entirely different view. R. E. Roberts asserts that he 'cannot agree with, the opinion that puts his last play in a definitely inferior position to his other work'.[26] Una Ellis-Fermor claims that these plays 'represent between them some of the noblest thought and the finest dramatic art in the whole of his work'.[27] Shaw, too, is of the same opinion. 'Here', he declares, 'the quintessence of Ibsenism reaches its final distillation; morality and reformation give place to mortality and resurrection'.[28] The truth of the matter is that these plays mark the ultimate stage of Ibsen's journey on the road to self-discovery and self-realization. They may not be theatrically as striking as his earlier plays,[29] but they are definitely far deeper and more significant. In them Ibsen carries his enquiry to a point where it is almost impossible to express

---

22 *Ibsen the Norwegian*, p. 124.

23 *Ibsen's Dramatic Technique*, pp. 87–88.

24 Op. cit., p. 125.

25 *Masters of the Drama*, pp. 380 and 379 respectively.

26 *Henrik Ibsen: A Critical Study*, p. 37.

27 Introduction to Ibsen's *The Master Builder and Other Plays*, p. 8.

28 *Major Critical Essays*, p. 91.

29 Although James Joyce wrote an enthusiastic article on *When We Dead Awaken* in the *Fortnightly Review* of April 1900, pleading for stage-worthiness of these plays: 'If any plays demand a stage they are the plays of Ibsen' (cited, J. W. McFarlane, *Ibsen and the Temper of Norwegian Literature*, p. 72).

oneself except through symbols. At the same time, he attains in these plays 'the completion of the artistic form toward which he had been, striving in the last years'.[30] As H. Koht continues, 'He who had once seemed the great master of naturalism in the theatre had now become the symbolic writer above all others. In truth, all his writing had carried within itself a symbolism, which more and more strongly had pressed its way forward, most strongly of all when he took his drama subjects only from his own soul. Then the words lost more and more the tone of the struggle and reality around him, then a submerged meaning seemed to quiver in each everyday word.'[31] This is precisely the kind of writing that the Swedish dramatist, August Strindberg (1849–1912), practised in his dramas and carried to even farther limits.

It is essential to take into account these different stages of Ibsen's growth as a dramatist, for he has often been identified only with the third stage of his writing—the social or realist drama. We must clearly remember that all the phases of his writing carry a significance of their own, and are equally important. They remind us that Ibsen's genius was multidimensional and a growing phenomenon, and that it cannot be confined to a single formula or formulation. As C. M. Bradbrook warns us, 'To see Ibsen merely as the precursor of Shaw and Brieux when he was also the precursor of Strindberg and Tchekov is to retain at this late date the false perspective of his contemporary critics and admirers.'[32]

III. IBSEN AND THE SOCIAL DRAMA

As *A Doll's House* belongs to Ibsen's so-called social or realistic drama, it will be worthwhile to dwell a little more on the nature and scope of the plays of this group. These plays, written in prose, include *The League of Youth* (1869), *Pillars of Society* (1877), *A Doll's House* (1879), *Ghosts* (1881) and *An Enemy of the People* (1882). They

[30] H. Koht, *The Life of Ibsen*, II, p. 323.

[31] Ibid., II, p. 323.

[32] *Ibsen the Norwegian*, p. 2.

proved the most influential of Ibsen's plays,[33] and established him as a great social reformer and moral teacher. 'This is the Ibsen', writes Eric Bentley, 'that scandalized Europe, the Ibsen that chimed with the Zolaist temper of the younger generation, the Ibsen of the *avant-garde* theatres of the nineties, the Ibsen, in a word, of Ibsenism, championed by Bernard Shaw for its positive values in *The Quintessence of Ibsenism*, and satirized by Bernard Shaw for the less sincere goings-on of its adherents in his first original comedy, *The Philanderer*.'[34]

In these plays Ibsen deals with contemporary social issues such as the place of women (*A Doll's House*), the taboo subjects of venereal disease and incest (*Ghosts*), the hypocrisies of middle-class gentility (*Pillars of Society*), or a community's incapacity to face the truth (*An Enemy of the People*). The plays follow the outward form of the well-made play that had been pioneered by Eugene Scribe, but depart from their model in offering credible, original characters and a serious view of society. In this repect Ibsen was, to some extent, influenced by the Danish scholar, Georg Brandes (1842–1927), who had exhorted him to take up the questions affecting the lives of ordinary men and women, and submit them to debate.[35] It is, in fact, in respect of these plays that Shaw's famous statement is specifically true:

> Shakespeare had put ourselves on the stage but not our situations. Our uncles seldom murder our fathers, and cannot legally marry our mothers; we do not meet witches; our kings are not as a rule stabbed and succeeded by their stabbers; and when we raise money by bills we do not promise to pay pounds of our flesh. Ibsen supplies the want left by Shakespeare. He gives us not only ourselves, but ourselves in our situations. The things that happen to his stage figures are things that happen to us.[36]

---

[33] George Steiner (*The Death of Tragedy*, p. 297) observes: 'Where Ibsen has been influential, as in the case of Shaw, it is the programmatic plays that have counted, not the harrowing dramas of his maturity.'

[34] *The Playwright as Thinker*, p. 92.

[35] See Brian W. Downs, *Ibsen: The Intellectual Background*, p. 143.

[36] 'The Quintessence of Ibsenism', *Major Critical Essays*, p. 144.

It should, however, be remembered that Ibsen was not the originator of 'social drama' (*drame sociale*), which was already made popular by the French dramatists Alexandre Dumas the Younger (1824–95) and Emile Augier (1820–89). In his own country he was preceded by Björnstjerne Björnson (1832–1910), whose plays like *The Newly-Weds* (1865) or *The Editor* (1874) were not only written in prose but raised also the questions of conduct applicable to many members of the public. Yet, as John Gassner points out, the main interest of Dumas, Augier and other Pre-Ibsenite playwrights was 'to defend middle-class interests and morals. If "ideas" functioned in their plays at all, they were conventional ones.[37] Ibsen, for the first time, turned the social drama into "the drama of ideas".'[38] He questioned, in these plays, the settled ideals, beliefs, and opinions which governed the life of his society and its members. As Shaw puts it, 'The drama arises through a conflict of unsettled ideals rather than through vulgar attachments, rapacities, generosities, resentments, ambitions, misunderstandings, oddities and so forth as to which no moral question is raised.'[39]

However, there is little justification for labelling these plays as 'thesis' (*pièce à thèse*), 'doctrinaire' or'programmatic' plays. Ibsen does not offer any clear-cut solutions or remedies for the evils he spotlights. Though many critics, like Shaw, have tried to codify his message, 'it turns out', as James W. McFarlane points out, 'that any generalization once made seems to demand reservation and qualification so drastic that the end result is little short of flat contradiction'.[40] Even Shaw, who has written the most assertive book about Ibsen, disarmingly admits the folly of making any confident assertion about his work: 'The conflict is not between clear right and wrong: the villain is as conscientious as the hero, if not more so: in fact, the question which makes the play interesting (when it

---

37 'Shaw on Ibsen and the Drama of Ideas', *Ideas in the Drama*, edited by John Gassner, p. 85.

38 Vivian Mercier, in his paper on 'From Myth to Ideas—and Back', remarks: 'The drama of ideas ought really to be called the drama of ideals for it presents not one isolated idea pitted against another but a conflict of opposing world views or ideologies' (*Ideas in the Drama*, p. 46).

39 Op. cit., p. 139.

40 *Ibsen and the Temper of Norwegian Literature*, p. 61.

is interesting) is which is the villain and which the hero'.[41] Ibsen himself has made it quite clear that his purpose was not to teach a lesson or propound a thesis. 'I do but ask', he declared, 'My call is not to answer.'[42] In fact, as J. Lavrin puts it succinctly, 'Ibsen's "ideas" are not those of a propagandist but of a seeker, who is on the look-out for the best artistic expression of truth "inherent" in life. They are those of a fighter, anxious to undermine—not as a preacher but again as artist—the old dead values which still continue to encumber, like ghosts, our lives.'[43]

Had Ibsen aimed at using these plays merely as vehicles for his ideas, they would have by now become outdated.[44] For, their ideas are no longer striking or revolutionary.[45] But the fact that the plays still continue to hold our interest shows clearly that they have got more than topical or polemical significance. Concerned apparently with contemporary and transitory issues, they are, like all truly great plays, the works of universal significance and great artistic power. '...instead of pamphlets on feminine mentality, the nature of marriage, or the unnerving influence of the sea, Ibsen presented the world with such creations as Nora Helmer, Oswald and Mrs. Alving, and the morbidly maladjusted wife Ellida Wangel—all of them as clear-cut and concrete as they could be'.[46] In fact, the plays are more a triumph of dramatic art than of ideas.[47]

---

41 Op. cit., p. 139.

42 Cited, H. Koht, *The Life of Ibsen*, I, 4.

43 *Ibsen: An Approach*, p. 21.

44 J. M. Synge, reacting to Shavian Ibsenism, believed actually that Ibsen had become outdated. He writes in his preface to *The Tinker's Wedding* (1907): 'Analysts with their problems and teachers with their systems are soon as old fashioned as the pharmacopoeia of Gelen—look at Ibsen and the Germans...'

45 H. L. Mencken maintains that Ibsen's ideas were not original or novel even in his own times. See his introduction to *Eleven Plays of Henrik Ibsen* (New York: The Modern Library, n.d.), pp. ix–x.

46 Janko Lavrin, *Ibsen: An Approach*, p. 24. Ibsen himself, apropos of his most intellectual drama, *Emperor and Galilean*, has observed: 'I look at the characters, at the conflicting designs, at history, and do not concern myself with the moral of it at all' (Cited, ibid., p. 25).

47 In this connections Vivian Mercier's remark is worth remembering: 'The great problem for the dramatist of ideas lies in the drama rather than in the ideas. If he cannot create interesting characters who embody in their own conflicts the conflicts of ideas or ideals, his work will satisfy neither actors nor audience' (*Ideas in the Drama,* p. 57).

These plays are also characterized as 'realistic' plays, but here, too, one has to remember that his realism is of a special kind. It is vitally different from the realism of the naturalistic writers like Émile Zola (1840–1902). As P. F. D. Tennant points out, 'Ibsen's realism, which gave the great impulse to the realist drama of modern times, always remained only an approximation to contemporary life, and never descended to the unpoetic drabness of the naturalistic school and that of his own numerous imitators.'[48] In fact, the charisma of his art lies in creating 'an illusion of realism', for Ibsen, as Eric Bentley asserts, 'remained to the end an arch-romanticist'.[49] 'He may depict scenes of middle-class life, but the creatures who inhabit these scenes are not of the middle range of humanity. When we think of them we think of human beings *possessed.*'[50] Beneath the realistic surface of contemporary characters, contemporary dialogue and a contemporary indoor setting, there lurks the world of 'the trolls and devils of *Peer Gynt,* that is to say, the trolls and devils of Norse folk tale'.[51] Perhaps the best description of Ibsen's realism comes from one of his own characters. What Rubek says of the realism of his portrait busts applies equally to Ibsen's realistic plays.

> Only I can see it—and how it makes me laugh! On the surface, there's the 'striking likeness', as they call it, that they all stand and gape with wonder at [lowering his voice]. But deep down underneath, there's the pompous self-righteous face of a horse, the obstinate muzzle of a mule... And it's these equivocal works of art that our worthy celebrities come and commission from me—and pay for in good faith... .[52]

In fact, Ibsen's'realism was greatly tempered by his use of romantic symbolism. As John Northam clearly demonstrates, 'much of the apparent realism in these plays is symbolic'.[53]

---

48 *Ibsen's Dramatic Technique*, p. 14.

49 *The Playwright as Thinker*, p. 94.

50 Allardyce Nicoll, *World Drama*, pp. 545-46.

51 Eric Bentley op. cit., p. 93.

52 *When We Dead Awaken,* Act I, *in Ghosts and other Plays,* tr. Peter Watts (Penguin Books, 1977), p. 229.

53 *Ibsen's Dramatic Method,* p. 13. Eric Bentley, too, asserts that 'nearly every "naturalistic" play of Ibsen's contains a central symbol whose significance spreads over the whole play' (op. cit., p. 98).

The plays, as such, should be valued not for their realism or ideas (which are generally borrowed from contemporary thinkers like John Stuart Mill, Darwin, or Kierkegaard) but for the skill with which Ibsen creates an illusion of realism or transmutes 'the borrowed trappings of contemporary thought'[54] into an exciting dramatic experience.

IV. IBSEN'S DRAMATIC ART

When Ibsen started play-writing the ruling dramatist of the day was Augustine Eugene Scribe (1791–1861), the French dramatist, whose 'well-made' (*pièce bien faite*) or 'intrigue' plays had formed the staple fare at Bergen and Christiania theatres during his stay there. The main interest of these plays lay in their plots which were skilfully constructed, and which kept the audience in a state of suspense and excitement till the very end. A number of tricks were used to serve this purpose—mistaken identity, misunderstandings, guilty secrets, lost letters, calculated exits and entrances, and so forth. Ibsen used almost all these expedients in his early plays and, though he gradually dispensed with them, retained till the close of his dramatic career some of the basic techniques of the 'well-made' play. Like them, his plays are built round a secret, often a guilty one, which invests their action with dramatic suspense.

However, Ibsen's plays are fundamentally different from the 'well-made' drama of Scribe and his followers. Unlike the latter, which simply aimed at amusement and recreation,[55] his plays were intended to arouse and awaken the audience. They appeal to the intellect rather than the emotions, and lay their emphasis more on characterization than plot. As a well-known critic points out, they give 'the illusion of undistorted reality, enabling the playgoer to observe the characters, and ponder the ideas and implications of a

[54] P. F. D. Tennant, op. cit., p. 120.

[55] Speaking of these plays, Raymond Williams, in his *Drama from Ibsen to Eliot*, remarks: 'Drama, in fact, had been reduced to a mere theatrical excitement. Character and action, which in the best Elizabethan drama had been primarily conventions for the expression of a larger dramatic experience, had become absolute theatrical qualities' (p. 51).

drama instead of watching the gyrations of the plot'.[56] In fact, Ibsen raised the drama from the level of pure entertainment to that of an effective means of self-discovery and enlightenment. 'Hence forth', says John Gassner, 'a playwright was not to expect honor for merely cooking up a stew of a plot; and although many a practitioner has continued' to acquire riches and a pretty reputation by no other means, a new standard of excellence was established'.[57]

A typical Ibsenian play is not so much unravelling of a plot as the revelation of character. Ibsen gradually reduces external action to such an extent that it almost becomes static. As H. Granville-Barker suggests, his plays may be called 'a drama rather of being than doing'.[58] In their structure, they resemble Greek drama more than Shakespearean or 'well-made' plays. Like the Greek playwrights, Ibsen uses the retrospective method by which a situation is developed rather than a story told. His plays open just before the catastrophe, and the preceding events are recalled rather than represented on the stage. His skill lies in his manipulating the threads of his plot in such a way 'that each revelation of the past is linked (by cause or effect) to some turn in the revelation of character which forwards the immediate action of the play'.[59]

Ibsen employed this method, for the first time, in his historical play, *The Vikings in Helgeland* (1858), but he dropped it afterwards and did not use it again until 1877 with *Pillars of Society*. Henceforth, with the sole exception of *An Enemy of the People*, it becomes the most dominating technique of his plays. P.F.D. Tennant describes beautifully how Ibsen applies it in a well-defined and set pattern:

> He presents first of all an idyllic picture of a household living its everyday life. Then this little fenced-in world is suddenly broken into by a visitor from the world outside. He or she is an old friend of the family who has not been seen for several years. These meetings of old friends are the pivot of nearly all Ibsen's plays and they are followed up by a perfectly natural exchange of recollections and enquiries about the intervening period during which the friends have not seen one another.

[56] John Gassner, *Masters of the Drama*, p. 356.

[57] Ibid., p. 371.

[58] *On Dramatic Method*, p. 183.

[59] H. Granville-Barker, op. cit., p. 178.

It is these enquiries which open up old wounds and bring about catastrophe.[60]

This description is especially true of the method of *A Doll's House*.

Again, like the Greek dramatists, Ibsen insists on the observance of the unities and the fate-motif. Like them, he avoids sub-plots and restricts the number of characters to a bare minimum. All this proves to him of great advantage. As H. Granville-Barker observes, 'By simplifying the scheme of a play's visible action (its reminiscent action will be another matter), in its scenic setting, in the number of characters, in singleness of subject, he can make both its plan and atmosphere effective.'[61]

Another feature of Ibsen's plays, towards which Bernard Shaw has drawn our attention,[62] is their realism or 'commonness'; his subjects, characters, situations, and settings—all are familiar to his audience. This was also the practice of the Greek playwrights who invariably drew on familiar myths and legends. Ibsen departs from them in so far as he chooses his subjects from the world around him. Here, too, he abstains from employing those characters and situations which are exceptional or uncommon. Instead of dwelling on the fortunes of a Hamlet or King Lear, he prefers to deal with the problems of a Nora or Mrs. Alving. His plays represent average humanity and its concerns. This is one of the reasons why they have got such a fascination for their audiences; the latter read in them the stories of their own lives. As R. Ellis Roberts points out, Ibsen 'brought us all back... to the right view of dramatic life; he made his audiences part of his plays. We live in, not look at, a play by Ibsen'.[63]

There are also some technical factors which contribute to the apparent realism of his plays. They include detailed stage-directions, employment of everyday prose, and elimination of soliloquies and 'asides'. His stress on the visual concreteness of his settings and characters helps him greatly in making his plays look life-like.

As external action in his plays is gradually replaced by inner action, Ibsen comes to depend on dialogue for the success of his

---

60 *Ibsen's Dramatic Technique*, p. 92.

61 Granville-Barker, op. cit., p. 173.

62 See 'The Quintessence of Ibsenism,' *Major Critical Essays*, p. 144.

63 *Henrik Ibsen: A Critical Study*, p. 183.

plays. 'Discussion', as Bernard Shaw says, becomes his chief weapon. '...it so overspreads and interpenetrates the action that it finally assimilates it, making the play and discussion practically identical'.[64] To serve this purpose, he uses 'rhetoric, irony, argument, paradox, epigram, parable, the arrangement of haphazard facts into orderly and intelligent situations'.[65]

Ibsen's major problem, as H. Granville-Barker puts it, was 'to give an apparently commonplace form of speech all the dramatic force and, when need be, all the emotional suggestion that poetry could give'.[66] To a large extent, he succeeds in this mission. Eric Bentley demonstrates clearly how his ordinary-looking prose performs the functions of poetry:

An Ibsenite sentence performs four or five functions at once. It sheds light on the character speaking, on the character spoken to, on the character spoken about; it furthers the plot; it functions ironically in conveying to the audience a meaning different from that conveyed to the characters (and it is not merely that the characters say things which mean more to the audience than to them, but that they also say things which, as one senses, mean more to the characters than to the audience); finally, an Ibsenite sentence is part of the rhythmic pattern which constitutes the whole act... It is as rich in artifice as the verse of *Peer Gynt*. Its very naturalness is the final artifice, the art that conceals the art.[67]

Janko Lavrin, too, stresses 'Ibsen's capacity for conveying unspoken thought, together with its emotional and mental undercurrents'.[68] As he points out, Ibsen 'imparts to the dialogue itself a new dimension as it were—by deepening it into the parallel inner dialogue "between the lines", which often fills the simplest words and remarks with a second meaning'.[69] In fact, as we have observed earlier, there is always a substratum of poetry and symbolism in Ibsen's plays.

---

[64] Op. cit., p. 146.

[65] Bernard Shaw, op. cit., p. 146.

[66] Op. cit., p. 171.

[67] *The Playwright as Thinker,* p. 97.

[68] *Ibsen: An Approach,* p. 27.

[69] Ibid, p. 29.

Ibsen's outstanding success as an artist lies in the way he invests his plays with telling realism without sacrificing any of the advantages that a poetic dramatist like Aeschylus or Shakespeare enjoys.

V. IBSEN'S ACHIEVEMENT AS A DRAMATIST

The days are gone when Ibsen's plays were a sensation both on and off the stage, but this should not be taken as a sign of his decline and fall. His immediate success was rather a *succès de scandale*, and was based, as M.C. Bradbrook suggests, on 'a very small proportion of his work',[70] his so-called social dramas. It was his unorthodox treatment of social and moral problems of the day which first attracted his contemporaries, and created a kind of stir that we can hardly conceive today. Shaw's *Quintessence of Ibsenism*, written in 1891, records the contemporary impact of his plays, and shows clearly, what he meant to the intellectuals of his age. To them, he was a revolutionary thinker, a social and moral philosopher of great significance. As Shaw put it, it was 'his message and the need of it',[71] which drew them towards his plays, and which, according to them, constituted their real strength.

Such a critical stand was but natural in an age which was seething with the spirit of revolution and change. But, now, most of the ideas round which Ibsen's social plays were built have lost their topical interest. They have either been assimilated in our social system or rejected as outdated. The plays, as such, have lost their sensational appeal. However, this loss has been suitably recompensed by a growing recognition of Ibsen's technical excellence. As J. W. McFarlane aptly observes, 'His normal stock has slumped, but this has been balanced by the appreciation in the value attached to his craftsmanship, he maintains his position, it seems, although no longer a leader of opinion but rather as a technician of the highest order.'[72] This is exactly the view-point of P.F.D. Tennant, the author *of Ibsen's Dramatic Technique* (1948). He demonstrates persuasively that

[70] *Ibsen the Norwegian*, p. 2.

[71] 'The Quintessence of Ibsenism', *Major Critical Essays*, p. 6.

[72] *Ibsen and the Temper of Norwegian Literature*, p. 59.

Ibsen's 'ideas have not stood the test of time as well as the characters which enunciate them, but the dramatic effect of his technique is as fresh as ever'.[73] According to him, 'It is Ibsen's dramatic form, not his ideas, which constitute his great contribution to the theatre.'[74]

This view, which represents the post-Shavian approach, is certainly more satisfying than the earlier one that rested merely on Ibsen's ideas. Nevertheless, it fails to do full justice to Ibsen's achievement as a dramatist. For one thing, it ignores the fact that form alone does not make a play. It lays its stress entirely on the form to the utter neglect of the theme in the same manner as the earlier critics emphasized the theme at the cost of the form. In this respect, this view is no less extremist and lopsided than the earlier one. As J.W. McFarlane rightly points out, 'Ibsen has often found himself in post-Shavian criticism taken out of the company of Schopenhauer, Darwin and Nietzsche and associated rather with Scribe and Augier and Feuillet and Dumas *fils* and the tradition of the *pièce bien faite*.'[75] Of course, it was wrong to associate Ibsen with the thinkers and philosophers like Nietzsche but it is equally wrong to bring him down to the level of Scribe and his followers. Taken either just as a thinker or a craftsman, he occupies but an ordinary place.

In fact, his contribution to the drama is two-fold; it depends both on the theme and the form of his plays, or rather on their harmonious fusion. Though it is necessary to reject the old idea of Ibsen as a great crusader, we should not forget that he made his plays the vehicles of significant themes. This is why his plays differ from those of Scribe and his school, though the latter were no less skilfully constructed. Even when he seems most concerned with the transitory complexities and pressures of 'modern' life, he is dealing convincingly with eternal and universal themes. As Storm Jameson remarks, 'His search for the truths of soul makes his thought timeless. It belongs to past, present and future, as a search for the truth of social conditions cannot.'[76] However, he would not have become a great dramatist if he had not possessed the talent of an artist. He owes his success as much to his vision of truth as to his

---

73 *Ibsen's Dramatic Technique*, p. 15.

74 Ibid., p. 16.

75 Op. cit., p. 59.

76 *Modern Drama in Europe*, p. 107.

ability to give it an appropriate form. Or, if we use the word in its truly broad sense, we can say that Ibsen's triumph was the triumph of a really great artist. For, as R. Ellis Roberts says, 'It is precisely the artist who knows that the separation between Truth and Beauty is one of words, not of facts; that the schism lies not in the nature of things, but in the crooked will of misinterpreting man.[77]

Historically speaking, Ibsen's contribution to the field of drama has been exceptionally remarkable and far-reaching. He was both a pioneer and a trend-setter. With him, as George Steiner observes, 'the history of drama begins anew'.[78] However, the truth of these statements will not be clear unless they are read in conjunction with the following extract from another critic:

> During a considerable part of the eighteenth and nineteenth centuries the contemporary acted drama in England and America was both intellectually and artistically stagnant. From, shall we say, the death of Sheridan to the emergence of Oscar Wilde, no Englishman and no American of considerable talent devoted himself chiefly to writing plays. The theatre, though it was sometimes commercially flourishing, was generally considered as nonliterary as intellectually dead as it was artistically null.[79]

This is true not only of the drama of England and America but also of other countries, including France. It was Ibsen who restored it again to its earlier glory. In his hands, the drama becomes a serious art—a means of self-discovery and awakening rather than pure entertainment. As James Joyce said, his plays 'are so packed with thought. At some chance expression, the mind is tortured with some question, and in a flash long reaches of life are opened up in vista...'[80] In this respect, he has been followed by all later dramatists, from Bernard Shaw to Brecht and Sartre. Actually, what we call 'modern drama' dates from him. He established a new tradition of dramatic writing which, in one form or another, still, continues.

---

[77] *Henrik Ibsen: A Critical Study*, p. 15.

[78] *The Death of Tragedy*, p. 290.

[79] Joseph Wood Krutch, '*Modernism' in Modern Drama*, p. 3.

[80] Cited, J. W. McFarlane, *op. cit.*, p. 72.

Intrinsically, Ibsen's plays are notable for their intellectual and artistic appeal. Instead of being dry exercises in moral persuasion (of which Shaw is sometimes guilty), they possess 'that quality of magic, of ecstasy which makes the supreme artist: he evokes souls by his art, and his evocation produces independent spirits who show us not the author's ideas but the idea of life, illustrate the purpose and meaning of humanity'.[81] Ibsen's real talent lies in the skill with which he invests the ordinary subjects with extraordinary meanings. As Allardyce Nicoll rightly notes, 'While outwardly Ibsen's scenes are "ordinary" and materialistically conceived, inwardly they are extraordinary and at times breathe the atmosphere of Peer Gynt's adventures in the hobgoblin's court.'[82] This is exactly what gives his work greatness and enduring interest. We may or may not agree with Luigi Pirandello who placed him next to Shakespeare,[83] but there is no doubt that he is one of the greatest dramatists the world has ever produced.

****

[81] R. Ellis Roberts, *op. cit.*, p. 192.

[82] *World Drama*, p. 546.

[83] 'After Shakespeare I unhestitatingly place Ibsen first.' Cited, Eric Bentley, *The Playwright as Thinker*, p. 75.

INTRODUCTION TO *A DOLL'S HOUSE*

A Doll's House is probably the most famous and best-known of Ibsen's plays. As M.C. Bradbrook puts it, 'Ibsen for many years, and to some people even today, means the author of *A Doll's House*'.[1] In fact, it was this play which made him known all over the world.[2] As William Archer rightly observes, 'it is with *A Doll's House* that Ibsen enters upon his kingdom as a world-poet. He had done greater work in the past, and he was to do greater work in the future; but this was the play which was destined to carry his name beyond the limits of Scandinavia and even of Germany, to the remotest regions of civilisation'.[3] Its impact was immediate and cataclysmic. The play, as H. Koht tells us, 'was discussed with arguments and counter-arguments, in newspapers, in periodicals, in special books—in Norway, Denmark, Sweden, Finland and Germany. Ministers preached about it in the churches, people spoke of it in their homes and outside of them'.[4] Possibly no other book had ever created such a wide-spead stir and excitement. No doubt, its popularity was somewhat of a *succès de scandale,* but its effect was by no means transitory. Bernard Shaw testifies to its far-reaching influence on

---

[1] *Ibsen the Norwegian*, p. 78.

[2] H. Koht (*The life of Ibsen*, II, P. 151) writes: 'A German translation with the title *Nora* appeared in Reclam's *Universal-Bibliothek* even before the end of the year 1879, and was sold by the thousands. Later the book was translated in one country after the other—in Finland in 1880, in England in 1882, in Poland in 1882, in Russia in 1883, and in Italy in 1884. It was soon known throughout the whole world.'

[3] Introduction to *A Doll's House, The Collected Works of Henrik Ibsen* (London William Heinemann, 1919), vol. VII, pp. vii–viii.

[4] *The Life of Ibsen*, II, 152.

social life when he writes that 'Nora's revolt is the end of a chapter of human history. The slam of the door behind her is more momentous than the cannon of Waterloo or Sedan'.[5] Similarly, M. C. Bradbrook underlines its contribution to the course of dramatic literature. 'The strong divorce play and the social drama', he asserts, 'are alike descended from it. *A Doll's House* stands in relation to modern drama as Queen Victoria to the royal families of Europe'.[6]

Today, with a change in our social and moral values, the play has lost much of its popular appeal. As Vivian Mercier points out, 'the tension at the end of *A Doll's House* used to be generated by the audience's prejudice against the views expressed by Nora; now that most people take Nora's side, the last act has lost much of its power'.[7] But this does not deprive it of its intrinsic merit. Stripped of its tinsel as it is, the play can now be appreciated better as a work of dramatic art.

* * *

The seeds of *A Doll's House* may be found in *The League of Youth* (1869) where Selma's outburst in the third act almost epitomizes the theme of the later play:

> How I've longed to share your troubles! But if ever I asked about anything I was sent about my business with a clever joke. You dressed me like a doll, and played with me as they play with a child. Oh, it would have been so wonderful to suffer with you. I'm a serious person, with a longing for all the higher, more inspiring things in life.[8]

However, it took Ibsen ten years to work out this theme, and give it a suitable dramatic form. *A Doll's House* was finished late in September 1879, and brought out on 4 December 1879.

Ibsen made the following notes for the play (dated, 'Rome, 19.10.1878') which show clearly how he conceived it at first:

> There are two kinds of spiritual law, two kinds of conscience, one in man and another, altogether different, in woman. They

---

[5] *Dramatic Opinions and Essays*, II, p. 259.

[6] Op. cit., p. 76.

[7] 'From Myth to Ideas—and Back,' *Ideas in the Drama*, ed. John Gassner, p. 57.

[8] *A Doll's House and Other Plays*, tr. Peter Watts (Penguin Books, 1973), p. 93.

do not understand each other; but in practical life the woman is judged by man's law, as though she were not a woman but a man.

The wife in the play ends by having no idea of what is right or wrong; natural feelings on the one hand and belief in authority on the other have altogether bewildered her.

A woman cannot be herself in the society of the present day, which is an exclusively masculine society, with laws framed by men and with a judicial system that judges femine conduct from a masculine point of view.

She has committed forgery, and she is proud of it, for she did it out of love for her husband, to save his life. But this husband with his commonplace principles of honour is on the side of the law and regards the question with masculine eyes.

Spiritual conflicts. Oppressed and bewildered by the belief in authority, she loses faith in her moral right and ability to bring up children. Bitterness. A mother in modern society, like certain insects who go away and die when she has done her duty in the propagation of the race. Love of life, of home, of husband and children and family. Here and there a womanly shaking-off of her thoughts. Sudden return of anxiety and terror. She must bear it all alone. The catastrophe approaches, inexorably, inevitably. Despair, conflict and destruction.[9]

It is interesting to see how these seminal thoughts have been transmuted into the play. In fact, Ibsen had to work hard before he was able to give his play its final shape. We can have a good idea of his toil and workmanship if we just compare the published play with the extant draft material.[10]

* * *

Ibsen chose for his play one of the burning topics of the day: woman's place in society. In this choice he was no less influenced by his own

---

[9] *The Collected Works of Henrik Ibsen*, ed. William Archer (London; William Heinemann, 1912), Vol. XII pp. 91–92. The volume contains also a scenario, a few detached fragments of dialogue, and a complete draft of the play (pp. 92–182).

[10] For a comparative analysis, see William Archer's introduction, in *The Collected Works of Henrik Ibsen*, Vol. XII, pp. 10–13, and John Northam, *Ibsen's Dramatic Method*, pp. 31–36.

convictions than the growing movement for the emancipation of women.[11] In February 1879, he actually proposed at the Scandinavian Club that the women members, too, should have the power to vote, and was greatly incensed when his proposal was struck down.[12] However, the play was not written just to support or advocate feminism. Ibsen himself made it quite clear in a speech which he delivered on 26 May 1898 at a banquet of the Norwegian Society for the Woman's Cause.

> I thank you for drinking my health, but I must reject the honour of having consciously worked for the woman's cause. I am not even clear what the woman's cause really is. For me it has been an affair of humanity.[13]

In fact, his sympathetic attitude towards women was a by-product of his passionate belief in human freedom. As Brian W. Downs rightly observes, 'women afforded him specimens of humanity peculiarly trammelled by their conventional disabilities in the struggle for personal emancipation'.[14] He was drawn towards them simply because he felt that women in society were denied the rights and opportunities to grow like men-folk.

As a matter of fact, Ibsen, in this play, tries to explore the true basis of the man-woman relationship in one of its most intimate forms: marriage. As J. Lavrin puts it, 'What propaganda value there is in this play at all, concerns not feminism but those ethical and spiritual factors without which marriage remains a mere "living together".[15]

* * *

The plot of *A Doll's House* does not differ much from that of a typical intrigue play. The heroine, Nora, is guilty of committing forgery, for which she is being black-mailed by the villain, Krogstad. This she had done in order to save the life of her husband, but he, instead of appreciating her act, denounces her as a liar and criminal.

---

[11] See Brian W. Downs, *Ibsen: The Intellectual Background,* pp. 157–61, for an account of the feminist movement.

[12] For details, see H. Koht, op. cit., II, pp. 148–49.

[13] Cited, Brian W. Downs, *Ibsen: The Intellectual Background,* p. 160.

[14] Ibid., p. 162.

[15] *Ibsen: An Approach,* p. 79.

However, she is ultimately saved by the intervention of her old friend, Mrs Linde, who brings about a change in Krogstad's heart. But Nora does not stay with her husband; she leaves her home and children to learn the ways of the world. Save this act, there is nothing unusual about the plot. As Bernard Shaw remarks, 'Up to a certain point in the last act, *A Doll's House* is a play that might be turned into a very ordinary French drama by the excision of a few lines, and the substitution of a sentimental happy ending for the famous last scene'.[16] Actually, what distinguishes this play is the sudden turn that Nora takes near the end when she says: 'Sit down here, Torvald. You and I have a lot to say to one another' (P. 74). 'And it was by this new technical feature,' continues Bernard Shaw, 'this addition of a new movement, as musicians would say, to the dramatic form, that *A Doll's House* conquered Europe and founded a new school of dramatic art.'[17]

The plot, as it stands, suffers from some obvious improbabilities. John Gassner observes: 'Would even a sheltered woman like Nora lack the elementary knowledge that forgery was illegal? Given the character of a dependent wife, would she have failed to confess to her husband? Given this character, moreover, it is extremely improbable that she would have left him and, above all, her innocent children.'[18] Similarly, R.E. Roberts asserts that he has 'never met anyone yet, of the type conveniently called "man of the world", who did not consider the point about the forgery a storm in a tea-cup, and Torvald's behaviour over it as only explicable on the grounds that he was a cad'.[19] However, these observations depend largely on one's reading of these characters, and will change materially if we look at them in a different light. For instance, if we do not take Nora as childish and thoughtless as she appears to be, her actions will appear far less improbable. She could very well pretend her ignorance of law

---

[16] 'The Quintessence of Ibsenism', *Major Critical Essays*, p. 138. Ibsen, in fact, was prevailed upon by the German theatre-goers to substitute a happy ending. In this version, Nora is induced to look at her sleeping children for the last time; she breaks down and decides to stay. However, this ending was not included in printed editions.

[17] Ibid., p. 138.

[18] *Masters of the Drama*, p. 369.

[19] *Henrik Ibsen: A Critical Study*, pp. 106–7.

as she could play the role of a 'doll'. In fact, her whole conduct prior to her declaration of independence is an exercise in dissimulation, and it is only through her casual remarks that we get an inkling of her real character. As John Gassner himself admits, 'The woman in the doll's house was not intrinsically a doll; barring the initial forgery, she only pretended to be one, because this was expected of her.'[20] Hers is really a very complex character, made up of contradictory traits. She plays a dual role—that of 'a child and a heroic woman in one,'[21] and the reader or spectator, unless he is perceptive enough, is likely to lose sight of the less obvious side of her character. One will have to read between the lines in order to understand her fully. It will, then, be clear that, if needed, she could leave her husband and children as unhesitatingly as she forged the signature of her father. John Gassner, too, concedes that 'Nora's leaving house and children is not so outrageously incredible as it seems at first sight, Ibsen having very astutely planted an extenuating circumstance. Like so many of her comfortable sisters, Nora has had very little function in her own household; servants had managed everything, including the children, and they can continue to do so.'[22] But this could not be the deciding factor; what prompted Nora to take such a momentous decision was something else. She was bound to her husband by her trust in his love for her: once it was shattered, there was no point in her staying with him. Of course, her decision was facilitated by the thought that her children would be safe with the servants.

Similar is the case with Torvald Helmer. If we study him closely we will see that his behaviour at his discovery of Nora's forgery is perfectly in accord with his role as a self-conceited moralist. To him, who prized social respectability far more than human values, this revelation would have come as the crack of doom. He could hardly keep his temper. As John Gassner correctly observes, 'In terms of simple human drama Helmer's attitude toward his wife's error is real and Nora's shock at his stuffy and selfish behaviour genuine.'[23] Dramatically, too, such a scene is necessary, for it not only brings

---

[20] *Masters of the Drama,* p. 370.

[21] J. Lavrin, op. cit., p. 79.

[22] *Masters of the Drama,* p. 370.

[23] Ibid., p. 370.

the play to its climax but provides what Aristotle calls *Anagnoresis* (Discovery)[24]: 'Nora sees Torvald and sees herself.'[25]

* * *

Objections have been raised also against the relevance of two important minor characters—Mrs Linde and Dr Rank. Of these, Mrs Linde is probably more defensible. She fills the useful role of a confidante, and is instrumental in averting the crisis that faced the Helmers. Moreover, her situation, by way of contrast and similarity, helps greatly in illustrating Nora's predicament. Without having an idea of Mrs Linde's original situation we can hardly realize the full implication of Nora's last step, for she places herself in the same position that Mrs Linde had had at the opening of the play. As John Northam put sit, 'She will arrive at Mrs Linde's a second Mrs Linde.'[26]

Dr Rank, too, is no less significant. He serves a variety of useful functions. First, ,his loneliness and sad fate offer a theatrical contrast to the apparent happiness of the Helmers' home. Secondly, as Brian W. Downs remarks, 'He serves to point a moral. As in his body he suffers for the excesses of his father, so Nora's weakness of character derives from *her* father, and, together with her criminality, can be transmitted to her children.'[27] This point, however, is not of much aesthetic relevance. More important than this is the fact that Dr Rank functions as 'the visual counterpart of Nora's torturing thoughts of death'.[28] It is against the background of his coming death that Nora's final gesture assumes the character of painful renunciation. His presence helps in defining and deepening her tragedy.

* * *

M. C. Bradbrook, writing about Ibsen's craftsmanship, refers especially to his 'technique of interplay and implication'.[29] *A Doll's House* offers a good example of this technique. The whole play is built

---

[24] See Aristotle, *On the Art of Poetry,* tr. Ingram Bywater (Oxford: The Clarendon Press, 1954), pp. 47–48.

[25] M. C. Bradbrook, op. cit., pp. 84–85.

[26] *Ibsen's Dramatic Method,* p. 27.

[27] *A Study of Six Plays by Ibsen,* p. 136.

[28] John Northam, op. cit., p. 30.

[29] *Ibsen the Norwegian,* p. 78.

on irony, suggestion and implicit symbolism. More is implied than stated. The incidents, characters and dialogues—all are contrived in such a way that they conceal as much as they reveal. Unless one is discerning enough, one is likely to miss the artistic beauty as well as the full significance of the play. Just to give an example, the irony of Nora's condescending behaviour towards Mrs Linde becomes clear only at the end of the play when we find her in Mrs Linde's position. We have already pointed out how Ibsen employs parallels and contrasting situations to extend the dimension of his meaning. As John Northam shows,[30] even small items like the Christmas-tree and the macaroons have a symbolic significance of their own, and contribute greatly to the total effect of the play. Its prose only looks simple and straightforward; in essence it is as subtle and complex as poetry. The play gives enough evidence of 'Ibsen's capacity for conveying unspoken thought'.[31] The more closely one reads it, the more rewarding will the experience be.

****

[30] John Northam, op. cit,, pp. 16–31. Some of his remarks have been incorporated in the 'Notes'.

[31] J. Lavrin, *Ibsen: An Approach*, p. 27.

Chronological List of Ibsen's Plays

(As English versions sometimes differ, the original Norwegian titles are given in brackets.)

Catilina (*Catilina*)	1850
The Warrior's Barrow (*Kjaempehöjen*)	1850
St John's Eve (*Sancthansnatten*)	1853
Lady Inger of Östraàt (*Fru Inger til Östraàt*)	1855
The Feast at Solhaug (*Gildet paa Solhaug*)	1856
Olaf Liljekrans (*Olaf Liljekrans*)	1857
The Vikings in Helgeland (*Haermaendene paa Helgeland*)	1858
Love's Comedy (*Kjaerlighedens Komedie*)	1862
The Pretenders (*Kongs-emnerne*)	1863
Brand (*Brand*)	1866
Peer Gynt (*Peer Gynt*)	1867
The League of Youth (*De Unges Forbund*)	1869
Emperor and Galilean (*Kejser og Galilaeer*)	1873
Pillars of Society (*Samfundets Stötter*)	1877
A Doll's House (*Dukkehjem*)	1879
Ghosts (*Gengangere*)	1881
An Enemy of the People (*Folkefiende*)	1882
The Wild Duck (*Vildanden*)	1884
Rosmersholm (*Rosmersholm*)	1886
The Lady from the Sea (*Fuen fra Havet*)	1888
Hedda Gabler (*Hedda Gabler*)	1890
The Master Builder (*Bygmester Solness*)	1892
Little Eyolf (*Lille Eyolf*)	1894
John Gabriel Borkman (*John Gabriel Borkman*)	1896
When We Dead Awaken (*Naar Vi Döde Vaagner*)	1899

A Doll's House

Dramatis Personae

TORVALD HELMER

NORA, his wife

DOCTOR RANK

MRS LINDE

NILS KROGSTAD

HELMER'S three young children

ANNE, their nurse

A HOUSEMAID

A PORTER

(*The action takes place in* HELMER'S *house*)

ACT I

SCENE: *A room furnished comfortably and tastefully, but not extravagantly. At the back, a door to the right leads to the entrance-hall, another to the left leads to* HELMER'S *study. Between the doors stands a piano. In the middle of the left-hand wall is a door, and beyond it a window. Near the window are a round table, arm-chairs, and a small sofa. In the right-hand wall, at the farther end, another door; and on the same side, nearer the footlights, a stove, two easy chairs, and a rocking-chair; between the stove, and the door, a small table. Engravings on the walls; a cabinet with china and other* *small objects; a small book-case with well-bound books. The floors are carpeted, and a fire burns in the stove. It is winter.*

A bell rings in the hall; shortly afterwards the door is heard to open. Enter NORA *humming a tune and in high spirits. She is in outdoor dress and carries a number of parcels; these she lays on the table to the right. She leaves the outer door open after her, and through it is seen a* PORTER *who is carrying a Christmas-tree and a basket, which he gives to the* MAID *who has opened the door.*

NORA: Hide the Christmas-tree carefully, Helen. Make sure, the children don't see it till this evening, when it is decorated. (*To the* PORTER, *taking out her purse.*) How much?

PORTER: Six pence.

NORA: There is a shilling. No, keep the change. (*The* PORTER *thanks her, and goes out.* NORA *shuts the door. She is laughing to herself, as she takes off her hat and coat. She takes a packet of macaroons from her pocket and eats one or two; then goes cautiously to her husband's door and listens.*) Yes, he is in. (*Still humming, she goes to the table on the right.*)

HELMER (*calls out from his room*): Is that my little lark twittering out there?

NORA (*busy opening some of the parcels*): Yes, it is!

HELMER: Is it my little squirrel scurrying around?

NORA: Yes!

HELMER: When did my squirrel come home?

NORA: Just now. (*Puts the bag of macaroons into her pocket and wipes her mouth*) Come in here, Torvald, and see what I have bought.

HELMER: Don't disturb me. (*A little later, he opens the door and looks into the room, pen in hand.*) Bought, did you say? All these things? Has my little spendthrift been wasting money again?

NORA: Yes, but, Torvald, this year we really can let ourselves go a little. This is the first Christmas that we have not needed to economize.

HELMER: Still, you know, we can't spend money recklessly.

NORA: Yes, Torvald, we can be a wee bit more reckless now, can't we? Just a tiny wee bit! You are going to have a big salary and earn lots and lots of money.

HELMER: Yes, after the New Year; but then it will be a whole quarter before the salary is due.

NORA: Pooh! We can borrow till then.

HELMER: Nora! (*Goes up to her and takes her playfully by the ear.*) The same little featherbrain! Suppose, now, that I borrowed fifty pounds today, and you spent it all in the Christmas week, and then on New Year's Eve a slate fell on my head and killed me, and—

NORA (*putting her hands over his mouth*): Oh! don't say such horrid things.

HELMER: Still, suppose that happened—what then?

NORA: If that were to happen, I don't suppose I should care whether I owed money or not.

HELMER: Yes, but what about the people who had lent it?

NORA: Them? Who would bother about them? I shouldn't know who they were.

HELMER: That is like a woman! But seriously, Nora, you know what I think about that. No debt, no borrowing. There can be no freedom or beauty about a home life that depends on borrowing and debt. We two have kept bravely on the straight road so far, and we will go on the same way for the short time longer that there need be any struggle.

NORA (*moving towards the stove*): As you please, Torvald.

HELMER (*following her*): Come, come, my little skylark must not droop her wings. What is this? Is my little squirrel upset? (*Taking out his purse.*) Nora, what do you think I have got here?

NORA (*turning round quickly*): Money!

HELMER: There you are. (*Gives her some money.*) Do you think I don't know what a lot is wanted for housekeeping at Christmas-time?

NORA (*counting*): Ten shillings—a pound—two pounds! Thank you, thank you, Torvald; that will keep me going for a long time.

HELMER: Indeed it must.

NORA: Yes, yes, it will. But come here and let me show you what I have bought. And all so cheap! Look, here is a new suit for Ivar, and a sword; and a horse and a trumpet for Bob; and a doll and a doll's bed for Emmy—they are very plain, but anyway she will soon break them to pieces. And here are dress-lengths and handkerchiefs for the maids; old Anne ought really to have something better.

HELMER: And what is in this parcel?

NORA (*crying out*): No, no! you mustn't see that till this evening.

HELMER: Very well. But now tell me, you extravagant little person, what would you like for yourself?

NORA: For myself? Oh, I am sure I don't want anything.

HELMER: Yes, but you must. Tell me something reasonable that you would particularly like to have.

NORA: No, I really can't think of anything—unless, Torvald—

HELMER: Yes?

NORA (*playing with his coat buttons, and without raising her eyes to his*): If you really want to give me something, you might—you might—

HELMER: Well, out with it!

NORA (*speaking quickly*): You might give me money, Torvald. Only just as much as you can afford; and then one of these days I will buy something with it.

HELMER: But, Nora—

NORA: Oh, do! dear Torvald; please, please do! Then I will wrap it up in a beautiful gilt paper and hang it on the Christmas-tree. Wouldn't that be fun?

HELMER: What are little people called that are always wasting money?

NORA: Spendthrifts—I know. Let's do as you suggest. Torvald, and then I shall have time to think what I am most in need of. That is a very sensible plan, isn't it?

HELMER (*smiling*): Indeed it is—that is to say, if you were really to save out of the money I give you, and then really buy something for yourself. But if you spend it all on the housekeeping and any number of unnecessary things, then I merely have to pay up again.

NORA: Oh but, Torvald—

HELMER: You can't deny it, my dear little Nora. (*Puts his arm round her waist.*) It's a sweet little spendthrift, but she uses up a lot of money. It's almost unbelievable how expensive such little persons are!

NORA: You shouldn't say that. I do really save all I can.

HELMER (*laughing*): That's very true—all you can. But you can't save anything!

NORA (*smiling quietly and happily*): You haven't any idea how many expenses we skylarks and squirrels have, Torvald.

HELMER: You are an odd little soul. Very like your father. You always find some new way of wheedling money out of me, and, as soon as you have got it, it seems to melt in your hands. You never know where it has gone. Still, one must take you as you are. It's in the blood; for it is true that you can inherit these things, Nora.

NORA: Oh, I wish I had inherited many of father's qualities.

HELMER: And I would not wish you to be anything but just what you are, my sweet little skylark. But, you know, it strikes me that you are looking rather—what shall I say—rather uneasy today?

NORA: Do I?

HELMER: You do, really. Look straight at me.

NORA (*looks at him*): Well?

HELMER (*wagging his finger at her*): Hasn't Miss Sweet-Tooth been breaking rules in town today?

NORA: No; what makes you think that?

HELMER: Hasn't she paid a visit to the confectioner's?

NORA: No, I assure you, Torvald—

HELMER: Not been nibbling sweets?

NORA: No, certainly not.

HELMER: Not even taken a bite at a macaroon or two?

NORA: No, Torvald, I assure, you really—

HELMER: There, there, you know I was only joking.

NORA (*going to the table on the right*): I shouldn't think of going against your wishes.

HELMER: No, I am sure of that; besides, you gave me your word—(*Going up to her.*) Keep your little Christmas secrets to yourself, my darling. They will all be revealed tonight when the Christmas-tree is lit, no doubt.

NORA: Did you remember to invite Doctor Rank?

HELMER: No. But there is no need; he will come to dinner with us as a matter of course. However, I will ask him when he comes in this morning. I have ordered some good wine. Nora, you can't think how I am looking forward to this evening.

NORA: So am I! And how the children will enjoy themselves, Torvald!

HELMER: It is wonderful to feel that one has a perfectly safe job, and a big enough income. It's delightful to think of, isn't it?

NORA: It's wonderful!

HELMER: Do you remember last Christmas? For quite three weeks beforehand you shut yourself up every evening till long after midnight, making ornaments for the Christmas-tree, and all the other fine things that were to be a surprise to us. It was the dullest three weeks I ever spent!

NORA: I didn't find it dull.

HELMER (*smiling*): But there was precious little result, Nora.

NORA: Oh, you shouldn't tease me about that again. How could I help the cat's going in and tearing everything to pieces?

HELMER: Of course you couldn't, poor little girl. You had the best of intentions to please us tall, and that's the main thing. But it is a good thing that our hard times are over.

NORA: Yes, it is really wonderful.

HELMER: This time I needn't sit here and be dull all alone, and you needn't ruin your dear eyes and your pretty little hands—

NORA (*clapping her hands*): No, Torvald, I needn't any longer, need I! Its wonderfully lovely to hear you say so! (*Taking his arm.*) Now I will tell you how I have been thinking we ought to arrange things, Torvald. As soon as Christmas is over—(*A bell rings in the hall.*) There's the bell. (*She tidies the room a little.*) There's someone at the door. What a nuisance!

HELMER: If it is a caller, remember I am not at home.

MAID (*in the doorway*): A lady to see you, ma'am—a stranger.

NORA: Ask her to come in.

MAID (*to* HELMER): The doctor came at the same time, sir.

HELMER: Did he go straight into my room?

MAID: Yes, sir.

(HELMER *goes into his room. The* MAID *ushers in* MRS LINDE, *who is in outdoor clothes, and shuts the door.*)

MRS LINDE (*in a dejected and timid voice*): How do you do, Nora?

NORA (*doubtfully*): How do you do—

MRS LINDE: You don't recognize me, I suppose.

NORA: No, I don't know—yes, of course, I seem to—(*Suddenly*) Yes! Christine! Is it really you?

MRS LINDE: Yes, it is I.

NORA: Christine! To think of my not recognizing you! And yet how could I—(*In a gentle voice.*) How you have altered, Christine!

MRS LINDE: Yes, I have indeed. In nine, ten long years—

NORA: Is it so long since we met? I suppose it is. The last eight years have been a happy time for me, I can tell you. And so now you have come into the town, and have taken this long journey in winter—that was brave of you.

MRS LINDE: I arrived by steamer this morning.

NORA: To have some fun at Christmas-time, of course. How lovely! We'll have such fun together! But take off your things. You are not cold, I hope. (*Helps her.*) Now let's sit down by the stove, and be cosy. No, lake this arm-chair; I'll sit here in the rocking-chair. (*Takes her hands.*) Now you look like your old self again; it was only the first moment—You are a little paler, Christine, and perhaps a little thinner.

MRS LINDE: And much, much older, Nora.

NORA: Perhaps a little older; very, very little; certainly not much. (*Stops suddenly and speaks seriously.*) What a thoughtless creature I am, chattering away like this. My poor, dear Christine, do forgive me.

MRS LINDE: What do you mean, Nora?

NORA (*gently*): Poor Christine, you are a widow.

MRS LINDE: Yes; it is three years ago now.

NORA: Yes, I knew; I saw it in the papers. I assure you, Christine, I meant ever so often to write to you at the time, but I always put it off and something always prevented me.

MRS LINDE: I quite understand, dear.

NORA: It was very bad of me, Christine. Poor thing, how you must have suffered. And he left you nothing?

MRS LINDE: No.

NORA: And no children?

MRS LINDE: No.

NORA: Nothing at all, then.

MRS LINDE: Not even any sorrow or grief to live upon.

NORA (*looking incredulously at her*): But, Christine, is that possible?

MRS LINDE (*smiles sadly and strokes her hair*): It sometimes happens, Nora.

NORA: So you are quite alone. How dreadfully sad that must be. I have three lovely children. You can't see them just now. They are out with their nurse. But now you must tell me all about it.

MRS LINDE: No, no; I want to hear about you.

NORA: No, you must begin. I mustn't be selfish today; today I must only think of your affairs. But there is one thing I must tell you. Do you know we have just had a great piece of good luck?

MRS LINDE: No, what is it?

NORA: Imagine, my husband has been made manager of the Bank!

MRS LINDE: Your husband? What good luck!

NORA: Yes, tremendous! A barrister's profession is such an uncertain thing, especially if he won't undertake unsavoury cases; and naturally Torvald has never been willing to do that, and I quite agree with him. You can imagine how pleased we are! He is to take up his work in the Bank at the New Year, and then he will have a big salary and lots of commissions. After this we can live quite differently—we can do just as we like. I feel so relieved and so happy, Christine! It will be wonderful to have heaps of money and no worries, won't it?

MRS LINDE: Yes, anyhow I think it would be delightful to have what one needs.

NORA: No, not only what one needs, but heaps and heaps of money.

MRS LINDE (*smiling*): Nora, Nora, haven't you learnt sense yet? At school you were always a great spendthrift.

NORA (*laughing*): Yes, that is what Torvald says now. (*Wags her finger at her*): But 'Nora, Nora' is not so silly as you think. We have not been in a position for me to waste money. We have both had to work.

MRS LINDE: You too?

NORA: Yes; odds and ends, needlework, crochet-work, embroidery, and that kind of thing. (*Dropping her voice.*) And other things as well. You know Torvald left his office when we were married? There was no prospect of promotion there, and he had to try and earn more than before. But during the first year he overworked himself dreadfully. You see, he had to make money every way he could, and he worked early and late; but he couldn't stand it, and became dreadfully ill, and the doctors said he must go south.

MRS LINDE: You spent a whole year in Italy, didn't you?

NORA: Yes. It was no easy matter to get away, I can tell you. It was just after Ivar was born; but naturally we had to go. It was a wonderfully beautiful journey, and it saved Torvald's life. But it cost a tremendous lot of money, Christine.

MRS LINDE: So I should think.

NORA: It cost about two hundred and fifty pounds. That's a lot, isn't it?

MRS LINDE: Yes, and in emergencies like that it is lucky to have the money.

NORA: I ought to tell you that we had it from father.

MRS LINDE: Oh, I see. It was just about that time that he died, wasn't it?

NORA: Yes; and do you know, I coudn't go and nurse him. I was expecting little Ivar's birth every day and I had my poor sick Torvald to look after. My dear, kind father—I never saw him again, Christine. That was the saddest time I have known since our marriage.

MRS LINDE: I know how fond you were of him. And then you went off to Italy?

NORA: Yes, you see we had money then, and the doctors insisted on our going, so we started a month later.

MRS LINDE: And your husband came back quite well?

NORA: As sound as a bell!

MRS LINDE: But—the doctor?

NORA: What doctor?

MRS LINDE: I thought your maid said the gentleman who arrived here just as I did was the doctor?

NORA: Yes, that was Doctor Rank, but he doesn't come here professionally. He is our greatest friend, and comes in at least once every day. No, Torvald has not had an hour's illness since then, and our children are strong and healthy and so am I. (*Jumps up and claps her hands.*) Christine! Christine! it's good to be alive and happy!—But how horrid of me; I am talking of nothing but my own affairs. (*Sits on a stool near her, and rests her arms on her knees.*) You mustn't be angry with me. Tell me, is it really true you did not love your husband? Why did you marry him? Why did you marry him?

MRS LINDE: My mother was alive then, and was bedridden and helpless, and I had to provide for my two younger brothers; so I did not think I was justified in refusing his offer.

NORA: No, perhaps you were quite right. He was rich at that time, then?

MRS LINDE: I believe he was quite well off. But his business was a precarious one; and when he died, it all went to pieces and there was nothing left.

NORA: And then?—

MRS LINDE: Well, I had to turn my hand to anything I could find—first a small shop, then a small school, and so on. The last three years have seemed like one long working-day, with no rest. Now it is ended, Nora. My poor mother needs me no more, she is gone; and the boys do not need me either; they have got jobs and can fend for themselves.

NORA: What a relief you must feel it—

MRS LINDE: No, indeed; I only feel my life unspeakably empty. No one to live for anymore. (*Gets up restlessly.*) That was why

I could not stand the life in my little backwater any longer. I hope it may be easier here to find something which will busy me and occupy my thoughts. If only I could be lucky enough to get some regular work—office work of some kind—

NORA: But, Christine, that is so frightfully tiring, and you look tired out now. You had far better go away to the seaside.

MRS LINDE (*walking to the window*): I have no father to give me money for a journey, Nora.

NORA (*rising*): Oh, don't be angry with me.

MRS LINDE (*going up to her*): It is you that must not be angry with me, dear. The worst of a position like mine is that it makes one so bitter. No one to work for, and yet obliged to be always on the look-out for chances. One must live, and so one becomes selfish. When you told me of the happy turn your fortunes have taken—you will hardly believe it—I was delighted not so much on your account as on my own.

NORA: How do you mean?—Oh, I understand. You mean that perhaps Torvald could get you something to do.

MRS LINDE: Yes, that was what I was thinking of.

NORA: He must, Christine. Just leave it to me; I will broach the subject very cleverly—I will think of something that will please him very much. It will make me so happy to be of some use to you.

MRS LINDE: How kind you are, Nora, to be so anxious to help me! It is doubly kind in you, for you know so little of the burdens and troubles of life.

NORA: I—I know so little of them?

MRS LINDE (*smiling*): My dear! Small household cares and that sort of thing!—You are a child, Nora.

NORA (*tosses her head and crosses the stage*): You ought not to be so superior.

MRS LINDE: No?

NORA: You are just like the others. They all think that I am incapable of anything really serious—

MRS LINDE: Come, come—

NORA: —that I have gone through nothing in this world of cares.

MRS LINDE: But, my dear Nora, you have just told me all your troubles.

NORA: Pooh!—those were trifles. (*Lowering her voice.*) I have not told you the important thing.

MRS LINDE: The important thing? What do you mean?

NORA: You look down upon me altogether, Christine—but you ought not to. You are proud, aren't you, of having worked so hard and so long for your mother?

MRS LINDE: Indeed, I don't look down on anyone. But it is true that I am both proud and glad to think that I was privileged to make the end of my mother's life almost free from care.

NORA: And you are proud to think of what you have done for your brothers.

MRS LINDE: I think I have the right to be.

NORA: I think so, too. But now, listen to this; I too have something to be proud and glad of.

MRS LINDE: I have no doubt you have. But what do you refer to?

NORA: Speak quietly. Suppose Torvald were to hear! He mustn't on any account—no one in the world must know, Christine, except you.

MRS LINDE: But what is it?

NORA: Come here. (*Pulls her down on the sofa beside her.*) Now I will show you that I too have something to be proud and glad of. It was I who saved Torvald's life.

MRS LINDE: 'Saved'? How?

NORA: I told you about our trip to Italy. Torvald would never have recovered if he had not gone there—

MRS LINDE: Yes, but your father gave you the necessary funds.

NORA (*smiling*): Yes, that is what Torvald and all the others think, but—

MRS LINDE: But—

NORA: Father didn't give us a shilling. I was the one who found the money.

MRS LINDE: You? All that large sum?

NORA: Two hundred and fifty pounds. What do you think of that?

MRS LINDE: But, Nora, how could you possibly do it? Did you win a prize in the Lottery?

NORA (*contemptuously*): In the Lottery? There would have been no credit in that.

MRS LINDE: But where did you get it from, then?

NORA (*humming and smiling with an air of mystery*): Hm, hm! Aha!

MRS LINDE: Because you couldn't have borrowed it.

NORA: Couldn't I? Why not?

MRS LINDE: No, a wife cannot borrow without her husband's consent.

NORA (*tossing her head*): Oh, if it is a wife who has any head for business—a wife who has the wit to be a little bit clever—

MRS LINDE: I don't understand it at all, Nora.

NORA: There is no need for you to. I never said I had borrowed the money. I may have got it some other way. (*Lies back on the sofa.*) Perhaps I got it from some other admirer. When anyone is as attractive as I am—

MRS LINDE: You are a mad creature.

NORA: Now, you know you're full of curiosity, Christine.

MRS LINDE: Listen to me, Nora dear. Haven't you been a little bit imprudent?

NORA (*sits up straight*): Is it imprudent to save your husband's life?

MRS LINDE: It seems to me imprudent, without his knowledge, to—

NORA: But it was absolutely necessary that he should not know! My goodness, can't you understand that? It was necessary he should have no idea what a dangerous condition he was in. It was to me that the doctors came and said that his life was in danger, and that the only thing to save him was to live in the south. Do you suppose I didn't try, first of all, to get what I wanted as if it were for myself? I told him how much I should love to travel abroad like other young wives; I tried tears and entreaties with him; I told him that he ought to remember the condition I was in, and that he ought to be kind and indulgent to me; I even hinted that he might raise a loan. That nearly made him angry, Christine. He said I was thoughtless, and that it was his duty as my husband not to indulge me in my whims and caprices—as I believe he called them. Very well, I thought, you must be saved—and that was how I came to devise a way out of the difficulty—

MRS LINDE: And did your husband never get to know from your father that the money had not come from him?

NORA: No, never. Father died just at that time. I had meant to let him into the secret and beg him never to reveal it. But he was so ill then—there never was any need to tell him.

MRS LINDE: And since then have you never told your secret to your husband?

NORA: Good heavens, no! How could you think I would? A man who has such strong views about these things! And besides, how painful and humiliating it would be for Torvald, with his manly independence, to know that he owed me anything! It would upset our mutual relations altogether; our beautiful happy home would no longer be what it is now.

MRS LINDE: Do you never mean to tell him about it?

NORA (*meditatively, and with a half smile*): Yes—some day, perhaps, after many years, when I am no longer as pretty as I am now. Don't laugh at me! I mean, of course, when Torvald is no longer as devoted to me as he is now; when my dancing and dressing-up and reciting have palled on him; then it may be a good thing to have something in reserve—(*Breaking off.*) What nonsense! That time will never come. Now, what do you think of my great secret, Christine? Do you still think I am useless? I can tell you, too, that this affair has been terribly worrying. It has been by no means easy for me to meet my commitments punctually. I may tell you that there is something that is called, in business, quarterly interest, and another thing called payment in instalments, and it is always so dreadfully difficult to manage them. I have had to save a little here and there, where I could, you understand. I haven't been able to put aside much from my housekeeping money, for Torvald likes good food. I couldn't let my children be shabbily dressed; I have felt I must use up all he gave me for them, the sweet little darlings!

MRS LINDE: So it has all had to come out of your own necessaries of life, poor Nora?

NORA: Of course. Besides, I was the one responsible for it. Whenever Torvald has given me money for new dresses and things like that, I have never spent more than half of it; I have always bought the simplest and cheapest things. Thank Heaven, any clothes look well on me, and so Torvald has never noticed it. But it was often very hard on me, Christine—because it is so nice to be really well dressed, isn't it?

MRS LINDE: Yes, of course.

NORA: Well, then I have found other ways of earning money. Last winter I was lucky enough to get a lot of copying to do; so I locked myself up and sat writing every evening until quite late at night. Often I was desperately tired; but all the same it was a tremendous pleasure to sit there working and earning money. It was like being a man.

MRS LINDE: How much have you been able to pay off in that way?

NORA: I can't tell you exactly. You see, it is very difficult to keep an account of a business matter of that kind. I only know that I have paid every penny that I could scrape together. Quite often I was at my wits' end. (*Smiles.*) Then I used to sit here and imagine that a rich old gentleman had fallen in love with me—

MRS LINDE: What! Who was it?

NORA: Be quiet—that he had died; and that when his will was opened it contained, written in big letters, the instruction: 'The lovely Mrs Nora Helmer is to have all I possess paid over to her at once in cash.'

MRS LINDE: But, my dear Nora—who could the man be?

NORA: Good gracious. can't you understand? There was no old gentleman at all; it was only something that I used to sit here and imagine, when I couldn't think of any way of procuring money. But it doesn't matter now; the tiresome old man can stay where he is, as far as I am concerned; I don't bother about him or his will either. I am free from care now. (*Jumps up.*) My goodness, it's wonderful to think of, Christine! Free from care! To be able to be free from care, quite tree from care; to be able to play and romp with the children: to be able to keep the house beautifully and have everything just as Torvald likes it. And think of it, soon the spring will come and big blue sky! Perhaps we shall be able to take a little trip—perhaps I shall see the sea again! Oh, it's a wonderful thing to be alive and be happy. (*A bell is heard in the hall.*)

MRS LINDE (*rising*): There is the bell; perhaps I had better go.

NORA: No, don't go; no one will come in here; it is sure to be for Torvald.

SERVANT (*at the hall door*): Excuse me, ma'am—there is a gentleman to see the master, and as the doctor is with him—

NORA: Who is it?

KROGSTAD (*at the door*): It is I, Mrs Helmer. (MRS LINDE *starts, trembles, and turns to the window.*)

NORA (*takes a step towards him, and speaks in a strained, low voice*): You? What is it? What do you want to see my husband about?

KROGSTAD: Bank business—in a way. I have a small post in the Bank, and I hear your husband is to be our chief now—

NORA: Then it is—

KROGSTAD: Nothing but dry business matters, Mrs Helmer; absolutely nothing else.

NORA: Will you please go into the study, then. (*She bows indifferently to him and shuts the door into the hall; then comes back and makes up the fire in the stove.*)

MRS LINDE: Nora—who was that man?

NORA: A lawyer, of the name of Krogstad.

MRS LINDE: Then it really was he.

NORA: Do you know the man?

MRS LINDE: I used to—many years ago. At one time he was a solicitor's clerk in our town.

NORA: Yes, he was.

MRS LINDE: He has altered a lot.

NORA: He made a very unhappy marriage.

MRS LINDE: He is a widower now, isn't he?

NORA: With several children. There now, it is burning up. (*Shuts the door of the stove and moves the rocking-chair aside.*)

MRS LINDE: They say he carries on various kinds of business.

NORA: Really! Perhaps he does; I don't know anything about it. But don't let us think of business; it is so tiresome.

DOCTOR RANK (*comes out of* HELMER'S *study. Before he shuts the door he calls to him*): No, my dear fellow, I won't disturb you; I would rather go into your wife for a little while. (*Shuts the door and sees* MRS LINDE.) I beg your pardon; I am afraid I am disturbing you too.

NORA: No, not at all. (*Introducing him.*) Doctor Rank, Mrs Linde.

RANK: I have often heard Mrs Linde's name mentioned here. I think I passed you on the stairs when I arrived, Mrs Linde?

MRS LINDE: Yes, I go up very slowly; I can't manage stairs well.

RANK: Ah! some slight internal weakness?

MRS LINDE: No, the fact is I have been overworking myself.

RANK: Nothing more than that? Then I suppose you have come to town to amuse yourself with our entertainments?

MRS LINDE: I have come to look for work.

RANK: Is that a good cure for overwork?

MRS LINDE: One must live, Doctor Rank.

RANK: Yes, the general opinion seems to be that it is necessary.

NORA: Look here, Doctor Rank—you know you want to live.

RANK: Certainly. However wretched I may feel, I want to prolong the agony as long as possible. All my patients are like that. And so are those who are morally diseased; one of them, and a bad case too, is at this very moment with Helmer—

MRS LINDE (*sadly*): Ah!

NORA: Whom do you mean?

RANK: A lawyer by the name of Krogstad, a fellow you don't know at all. He suffers from a diseased moral character, Mrs Helmer; but even he began talking of its being highly important that he should live.

NORA: Did he? What did he want to speak to Torvald about?

RANK: I have no idea; I only heard that it was something about the Bank.

NORA: I didn't know this—what's his name—Krogstad had anything to do with the Bank.

RANK: Yes, he has some sort of post there. (*To* MRS LINDE.) I don't know whether you find also in your part of the world that there are certain people who go zealously snuffing about to smell out moral corruption, and, as soon as they have found some, put the person concerned into some lucrative position where they can keep their eye on him. Healthy natures are left out in the cold.

MRS LINDE: Still I think the sick are those who most need taking care of.

RANK (*shrugging his shoulders*): Yes, there you are. That is the sentiment that is turning society into a sick-house.

(NORA, *who has been absorbed in her thoughts, breaks out into smothered laughter and claps her hands.)*

RANK: Why do you laugh at that? Have you any notion what society really is?

NORA: What do I care about silly old society? I am laughing at something quite different, something extremely amusing. Tell me, Doctor Rank, are all the people who are employed in the Bank dependent on Torvald now?

RANK: Is that what you find so extremely amusing?

NORA (*smiling and humming*): That's my affair! (*Walking about the room.*) It's perfectly glorious to think that we have—that Torvald has so much power over so many people. (*Takes the packet from her pocket.*) Doctor Rank, what do you say to a macaroon?

RANK: What, macaroons? I thought they were forbidden here.

NORA: Yes, but these are some Christine gave me.

MRS LINDE: What! I—

NORA: Oh, well, don't be alarmed! You couldn't know that Torvald had forbidden them. I must tell you that he is afraid they will spoil my teeth. But, gracious!—once in a way—That's so, isn't it, Doctor Rank? Excuse me! (*Puts a macaroon into his mouth.*) You must have one too, Christine. And I shall have one, just a little one—or at most two. (*Walking about.*) I am tremendously happy. There is just one thing in the world now that I should dearly love to do.

RANK: Well, what is that?

NORA: It's something I should dearly love to say, if Torvald could hear me.

RANK: Well, why can't you say it?

NORA: No, I daren't; it's so shocking.

MRS LINDE: Shocking?

RANK: Well, I should not advise you to say it. Still, with us you might. What is it you would so much like to say if Torvald could hear you?

NORA: I should just love to say—Well, I'm damned!

RANK: Are you mad?

MRS LINDE: Nora, dear—!

RANK: Say it, here he is!

NORA (*hiding the packet*): Hush! Hush! Hush! (HELMER *comes out of his room, with his coat over his arm and his hat in his hand.*)

NORA: Well, Torvald dear, have you got rid of him?

HELMER: Yes, he has just gone.

NORA: Let me introduce you—this is Christine, who has come to town.

HELMER: Christine—? I'm sorry, but I don't know—

NORA: Mrs Linde, dear; Christine Linde.

HELMER: Of course. A school friend of my wife's, I presume?

MRS LINDE: Yes, we have known each other since then.

NORA: And just think, she has come a long way in order to see you.

HELMER: What do you mean?

MRS LINDE: No, really, I—

NORA: Christine is tremendously clever at book-keeping, and she is frightfully anxious to work under some clever man, so as to perfect herself—

HELMER: Very sensible Mrs Linde.

NORA: And when she heard you had been appointed manager of the Bank—the news was telegraphed, you know—she travelled here as quick as she could. Torvald, I am sure you will be able to do something for Christine, for my sake, won't you?

HELMER: Well, it is not altogether impossible. I presume you are a widow, Mrs Linde?

MRS LINDE: Yes.

HELMER: And have had some experience of book-keeping?

MRS LINDE: Yes, a fair amount.

HELMER: Ah! well, it's very likely I may be able to find something for you—

NORA (*clapping her hands*): What did I tell you? What did I tell you?

HELMER: You have just come at a fortunate moment, Mrs Linde.

MRS LINDE: How am I to thank you?

HELMER: There is no need. (*Puts on his coat.*) But today you must excuse me—

RANK: Wait a minute; I will come with you. (*Brings his fur coat from the hall and warms it at the fire.*)

NORA: Don't be away long, Torvald dear.

HELMER: About an hour, not more.

NORA: Are you going too, Christine?

MRS LINDE (*putting on her cloak*): Yes, I must go and look fcr a room.

HELMER: Oh, well then, we can walk down the street together.

NORA (*helping her*): What a pity it is we are so short of space here;

MRS LINDE: Please don't think of it! Good-bye, Nora dear, and many thanks.

NORA: Good-bye for the present. Of course you will come back this evening. And you too, Dr Rank. What do you say? If you are well enough? Oh, you must be! Wrap yourself up well. (*They go to the door all talking together. Children's voices are heard on the staircase.*)

NORA: There they are! There they are! (*She runs to open the door. The* NURSE *comes in with the children.*) Come in! Come in! (*Stoops and kisses them.*) Oh, you sweet blessings! Look at them, Christine! Aren't they darlings?

RANK: Don't let us stand here in the draught.

HELMER: Come along, Mrs Linde; the place will only be bearable for a mother now!

(RANK, HELMER, *and* MRS LINDE *go downstairs. The* NURSE *comes forward with the children;* NORA *shuts the hall door.*)

NORA: How fresh and well you look! Such red cheeks!—like apples and roses. (*The children all talk at once while she speaks to them.*) Have you had great fun? That's splendid! What, you pulled both Emmy and Bob along on the sledge?—both at once?—that *was good.* You are a clever boy, Ivar. Let me take her for a little, Anne. My sweet little baby doll! (*Takes the baby from the* MAID *and dances it up and down.*) Yes, yes, mother will dance with Bob too. What! Have you been snowballing? I wish I had been there too! No, no, I'll take their things off, Anne; please let me do it, it is such fun. Go in now, you look half frozen. There is some hot coffee for you on the stove.

(*The* NURSE *goes into the room on the left,* NORA *takes off the children's things and throws them about, while they all talk to her at once.*)

NORA: Really! Did a big dog run after you? But it didn't bite you? No, dogs don't bite nice little dolly children. You mustn't look at the parcels, Ivar. What are they? Ah, I dare say you would like to know. No, no—it's something nasty! Come, let us have a game! What shall we play at? Hide and Seek? Yes, we'll play Hide and Seek. Bob shall hide first. Must I hide? All right, I'll hide first. (*She and the children laugh and shout, and romp in and out of the room; at last* NORA *hides under the table, the children rush in and out, looking for her, but do not see her; they hear her smothered laughter, run to the table, lift up the cloth, and find her. Shouts of laughter. She crawls forward and pretends to frighten them. Fresh laughter. Meanwhile there has been a knock at the hall door, but none of them has noticed it. The door is half opened, and* KROGSTAD *appears. He waits a little, the game goes on.*

KROGSTAD: Excuse me, Mrs Helmer.

NORA (*with a stifled cry, turns round and gets up on to her knees*): Oh! what do you want?

KROGSTAD: Forgive me, the outer door was ajar; I suppose someone forgot to shut it.

NORA (*rising*): My husband is out, Mr Krogstad.

KROGSTAD: I know that.

NORA: What do you want here, then?

KROGSTAD: A word with you.

NORA: With me?—(*To the children, gently.*) Go in to nurse. What? No, the strange man won't do mother any harm. When he has gone we will have another game. (*She takes the children into the room on the left, and shuts the door after them.*) You want to speak to me.

KROGSTAD: Yes, I do.

NORA: Today? It is not the first of the month yet.

KROGSTAD: No, it's Christmas Eve, and it will depend on you what sort of a Christmas you will spend.

NORA: What do you mean? Today it is absolutely impossible for me—

KROGSTAD: We won't talk about that till later on. This is something different. I presume you can give me a moment?

NORA: Yes, yes, I can—although—

KROGSTAD: Good. I was in Olsen's Restaurant and saw your husband going down the street—

NORA: Yes?

KROGSTAD: With a lady.

NORA: What then?

KROGSTAD: May I inquire if it was a Mrs Linde?

NORA: It was.

KROGSTAD: Just arrived in town?

NORA: Yes, today.

KROGSTAD: She is a great friend of yours, isn't she?

NORA: She is. But I don't see—

KROGSTAD: I know her too, once upon a time.

NORA: I am aware of that.

KROGSTAD: Are you? So you know all about it; I thought as much. Then I can ask you, without beating about the bush—is Mrs Linde to have a job in the Bank?

NORA: What right have you to question me, Mr Krogstad?—You, one of my husband's subordinates! But since you ask, you shall know. Yes, Mrs Linde *is* to have a job. And it was I who pleaded her cause, Mr Krogstad, let me tell you that.

KROGSTAD: I was right in what I thought, then.

NORA (*walking up and down the stage*)**:** Sometimes one has a tiny little bit of influence, I should hope. Because one is a woman, it does not necessarily follow that—when anyone is in a subordinate position, Mr Krogstad, they should really be careful to avoid offending anyone who— who—

KROGSTAD: Who has influence?

NORA: Exactly.

KROGSTAD (*changing his tone*)**:** Mrs Helmer; you will kindly use your influence on my behalf.

NORA: What? What do you mean?

KROGSTAD: You will kindly see that I am allowed to keep my subordinate position in the Bank.

NORA: What do you mean by that? Who proposes to take your post away from you?

KROGSTAD: Oh, there is no necessity to keep up the pretence of ignorance. I can quite understand that your friend is not very anxious to expose herself to the chance of rubbing shoulders with me; and I quite understand, too, whom I have to thank for being turned off.

NORA: But I assure you—

KROGSTAD: Very likely; but, to come to the point, the time has come when I should advise you to use your influence to prevent that.

NORA: But, Mr Krogstad, I *have* no influence.

KROGSTAD: Haven't you? I thought you said yourself just now—

NORA: Naturally I did not mean you to put that construction on it. I! What should make you think I have any influence of that kind with my husband?

KROGSTAD: Oh, I have known your husband from our student days. I don't suppose he is any more unassailable than other husbands.

NORA: If you speak slightingly of my husband, I shall turn you out of the house.

KROGSTAD: You are bold, Mrs Helmer.

NORA: I am not afraid of you any longer. As soon as the New Year comes, I shall be free of the whole thing in a very short time.

KROGSTAD (*controlling himself*): Listen to me, Mrs Helmer. If necessary, I am prepared to fight for my small job in the Bank as if I were fighting for my life.

NORA: So it seems.

KROGSTAD: It's not only for the sake of the money; as a matter of fact, that weighs least with me in the matter. There is another reason—well, I may as well tell you. My position is this. I dare say you know, like everybody else, that once, many years ago, I was guilty of an indiscretion.

NORA: I think I have heard something of the kind.

KROGSTAD: The matter never came into court; but every way seemed to be closed to me after that. So I took to the business that you know of. I had to do something; and, honestly, I don't think I've been one of the worst. But now I must cut myself free from all that. My sons are growing up; for their sake I must try and win back as much respect as I can in the town. This job in the Bank was like the first step up for me—and now your husband is going to kick me downstairs again into the mud.

NORA: But you must believe me, Mr Krogstad; it is not in my power to help you at all.

KROGSTAD: Then it is because you haven't the will; but I have means to compel you.

NORA: You don't mean that you will tell my husband that I owe you money?

KROGSTAD: Hm!—suppose I were to tell him?

NORA: It would be perfectly infamous of you. (*Sobbing.*) To think of his learning my secret, which has been my pride and joy, in such an ugly, clumsy way—that he should learn it from you! And it would put me in a horribly disagreeable position—

KROGSTAD: Only disagreeable?

NORA (*impetuously*): Well, do it, then!—and it will be the worse for you. My husband will see for himself what a blackguard you are, and you certainly won't keep your job then.

KROGSTAD: I asked you if it was only a disagreeable scene at home that you were afraid of?

NORA: If my husband does get to know of it, of course he will at once pay you what is still owing, and we shall have nothing more to do with you.

KROGSTAD (*coming a step nearer*): Listen to me, Mrs Helmer. Either you have a very bad memory or you know very little of business. I shall have to remind you of a few details.

NORA: What do you mean?

KROGSTAD: When your husband was ill, you came to me to borrow two hundred and fifty pounds.

NORA: I didn't know anyone else to go to.

KROGSTAD: I promised to get you that amount—

NORA: Yes, and you did so.

KROGSTAD: I promised to get you that amount, on certain conditions. Your mind was so taken up with your husband's illness, and you were so anxious to get the money for your journey, that you seem to have paid no attention to the conditions of our bargain. Therefore it will not be amiss if I remind you of them. Now, I promised to get the money on the security of a bond which I drew up.

NORA: Yes, and which I signed.

KROGSTAD: Good. But below your signature there were a few lines constituting your father a surety for the money; those lines your father should have signed.

NORA: Should? He did sign them.

KROGSTAD: I had left the date blank; that is to say, your father should himself have inserted the date on which he signed the paper. Do you remember that?

NORA: Yes, I think I remember—

KROGSTAD: Then I gave you the bond to send by post to your father. Isn't that so?

NORA: Yes.

KROGSTAD: And you naturally did so at once, because five or six days afterwards you brought me the bond with your father's signature. And then I gave you the money.

NORA: Well, haven't I been paying it off regularly?

KROGSTAD: Fairly regularly, yes. But—to come back to the matter in hand—that must have been a very trying time for you, Mrs Helmer?

NORA: It was, indeed.

KROGSTAD: Your father was very ill, wasn't he?

NORA: He was very near his end.

KROGSTAD: And died soon afterwards?

NORA: Yes.

KROGSTAD: Tell me, Mrs Helmer, can you by any chance remember what day your father died?—on what day of the month, I mean.

NORA: Father died on the 29th of September.

KROGSTAD: That is correct; I have ascertained it for myself. And, as that is so, there is a discrepancy (*taking a paper from his pocket*) which I cannot account for.

NORA: What discrepancy? I don't know—

KROGSTAD: The discrepancy consists, Mrs Helmer, in the fact that your father signed this bond three days after his death.

NORA: What do you mean? I don't understand—

KROGSTAD: Your father died on the 29th of September. But, look here; your father has dated his signature the 2nd of October. It is a discrepancy, isn't it? (NORA *is silent.*) Can you explain it to me? (NORA *is still silent.*) It is a remarkable thing, too, that the words '2nd of October,' as well as the year, are not written in your father's handwriting but in one that I think I know. Well, of course it can be explained; your father may have forgotten to date his signature, and someone else may have dated it haphazard before they knew of his death. There is no harm in that. It all depends on the signature of the name; and *that* is genuine, I suppose, Mrs Helmer? It was your father himself who signed his name here?

NORA (*after a short pause, throws her head up and looks defiantly at him*): No, it was not. It was I who wrote father's name.

KROGSTAD: Are you aware that is a dangerous confession?

NORA: In what way? You shall have your money soon.

KROGSTAD: Let me ask you a question; why did you not send the paper to your father?

NORA: It was impossible; father was so ill. If I had asked him for his signature, I should have had to tell him what the money was to be used for; and when he was so ill himself I couldn't tell him that my husband's life was in danger—it was impossible.

KROGSTAD: It would have been better for you if you had given up your trip abroad.

NORA: No, that was impossible. That trip was to save my husband's life; I couldn't give that up.

KROGSTAD: But did it never occur to you that you were committing a fraud on me?

NORA: I couldn't take that into account; I didn't trouble myself about you at all. I couldn't bear you, because you put so many heartless difficulties in my way, although you knew what a dangerous condition my husband was in.

KROGSTAD: Mrs Helmer, you evidently do not realize clearly what it is that you have been guilty of. But I can assure you that my one false step, which lost me all my reputation, was nothing more or nothing worse than what you have done.

NORA: You? Do you ask me to believe that you were brave enough to run a risk to save your wife's life?

KROGSTAD: The law cares nothing about motives.

NORA: Then it must be a very foolish law.

KROGSTAD: Foolish or not, it is the law by which you will be judged, if I produce this paper in court.

NORA: I don't believe it. Is a daughter not to be allowed to spare her dying father anxiety and care? Is a wife not to be allowed to save her husband's life? I don't know much about law; but I am certain that there must be laws permitting such things as that. Have you no knowledge of such laws—you who are a lawyer? You must be a very poor lawyer, Mr Krogstad.

KROGSTAD: Maybe. But matters of business—such business as you and I have had together—do you think I don't understand that? Very well. Do as you please. But let me tell you this—if

I lose my position a second time, you shall lose yours with me. (*He bows, and goes out through the hall.*)

NORA (*appears buried in thought for a short time, then tosses her head*): Nonsense! Trying to frighten me like that!—I am not as silly as he thinks. (*Begins to busy herself putting the children's things in order.*) And yet—? No, it's impossible! I did it for love's sake.

THE CHILDREN (*in the doorway on the left*): Mother, the stranger man has gone out through the gate.

NORA: Yes, dears, I know. But, don't tell anyone about the stranger man. Do you hear? Not even father.

CHILDREN: No, mother; but will you come and play again?

NORA: Yes, but I can't now. Run along in; I have such a lot to do. Run along in, my sweet little darlings. (*She gets them into the room by degrees and shuts the door on them; then sits down on the sofa, takes up a piece of needlework, and sews a few stitches, but soon stops.*) No! (*Throws down the work, gets up, goes to the hall door, and calls out.*) Helen! bring the tree in. (*Goes to the table on the left, opens a drawer, and stops again.*) No. no! it is quite impossible!

MAID (*coming in with the tree*): Where shall I put it, ma'am?

NORA: Here, in the middle of the floor.

MAID: Shall I get you anything else?

NORA: No, thank you. I have all I want. [*Exit* MAID

NORA (*begins decorating the tree*): A candle here—and flowers here—The horrible man! It's all nonsense—there's nothing wrong. The tree shall be marvellous! I will do everything I can think of to please you, Torvald!—I will sing for you, dance for you—(HELMER *comes in with some papers under his aim.*) Oh! are you back already?

HELMER: Yes. Has anyone been here?

NORA: Here? No.

HELMER: That's strange. I saw Krogstad going out of the gate.

NORA: Did you? Oh, yes, I forgot, Krogstad was here for a moment.

HELMER: Nora, I can see from your manner that he has been here begging you to say a good word for him.

NORA: Yes.

HELMER: And you were to appear to do it of your own accord; you were to conceal from me the fact of his having been here; didn't he beg that of you too?

NORA: Yes, Torvald, but—

HELMER: Nora, Nora, and you would be a party to that sort of thing? To have any talk with a man like that, and give him any sort of promise? And to tell me a lie into the bargain?

NORA: A lie—?

HELMER: Didn't you tell me no one had been here? (*Shakes his finger at her.*) My little song-bird must never do that again. A song-bird must have a clean beak to chirp with—no false notes! (*Puts his arm round her waist.*) That is so, isn't it? Yes, I am sure it is. (*Lets her go.*) We will say no more about it. (*Sits down by the stove.*) How warm and snug it is here! (*Turns over his paper.*)

NORA (*after a short pause, during which she busies herself with the Christmas-tree*): Torvald!

HELMER: Yes.

NORA: I am looking forward tremendously to the fancy-dress ball at the Stenborgs' the day after tomorrow.

HELMER: And I am tremendously curious to see what you are going to surprise me with.

NORA: It was very silly of me to want to do that.

HELMER: What do you mean?

NORA: I can't hit upon anything that will do; everything I think of seems so silly and insignificant.

HELMER: Does my little Nora acknowledge that at last?

NORA (*standing behind his chair with her arms on the back of it*): Are you very busy, Torvald?

HELMER: Well—

NORA: What are all those papers?

HELMER: Bank business.

NORA: Already?

HELMER: I have got authority from the retiring manager to undertake the necessary changes in the staff and in the rearrangement of the work; and I must make use of the Christmas week for that, so as to have everything in order for the new year.

NORA: Then that was why this poor Krogstad—

HELMER: Hm!

NORA (*leans against the back of his chair and strokes his hair*): If you hadn't been so busy I should have asked you a tremendously big favour, Torvald.

HELMER: What is that? Tell me.

NORA: There is no one has such good taste as you. And I do so want to look nice at the fancy-dress ball. Torvald, couldn't you take me in hand and decide what I shall go as, and what sort of a dress I shall wear?

HELMER: Aha! so my obstinate little woman is obliged to get someone to come to her rescue?

NORA: Yes, Torvald, I can't get along a bit without your help.

HELMER: Very well, I will think it over, we shall manage to hit upon something.

NORA: That is nice of you. (*Goes to the Christmas-tree. A short pause.*) How pretty the red flowers look—But, tell me, was it really something very bad that this Krogstad was guilty of?

HELMER: He forged someone's name. Have you any idea what that means?

NORA: Isn't it possible that he was driven to do it by necessity?

HELMER: Yes; or, as in so many cases, by imprudence. I am not so heartless as to condemn a man altogether because of a single false step of that kind.

NORA: No, you wouldn't, would you, Torvald?

HELMER: Many a man has been able to retrieve his character, if he has openly confessed his fault and taken his punishment.

NORA: Punishment—?

HELMER: But Krogstad did nothing of that sort; he got himself out of it by a cunning trick, and that is why he has gone under altogether.

NORA: But do you think it would—?

HELMER: Just think how a guilty man like that has to lie and play the hypocrite with everyone, how he has to wear a mask in the presence of those near and dear to him, ever before his own wife and children. And about the children—that is the most terrible part of it all, Nora.

NORA: How?

HELMER: Because such an atmosphere of lies infects and poisons the whole life of a home. Each breath the children take in such a house is full of the germs of evil.

NORA (*coming nearer him*): Are you sure of that?

HELMER: My dear, I have often seen it in the course of my life as a lawyer. Almost everyone who has gone to the bad early in life has had a deceitful mother.

NORA: Why do you only say—mother?

HELMER: It seems most commonly to be the mother's influence, though naturally a bad father's would have the same result. Every lawyer is familiar with the fact. This Krogstad, now, has been persistently poisoning his own children with lies and dissimulation; that is why I say he has lost all moral character. (*Holds out his hands to her.*) That is why my sweet little Nora must promise me not to plead his cause. Give me your hand on it. Come, come, what is this? Give me your hand. There now, that's settled. I assure you it would be quite impossible for me to work with him; I literally feel physically ill when I am in the company of such people.

NORA (*takes her hand out of his and goes to the opposite side of the Christmas-tree*): It's terribly hot in here; and I have such a lot to do.

HELMER (*getting up and putting his papers in order*): Yes, and I must try and read through some of these before dinner; and I must think about your costume, too. And it is just possible I may have something ready in gold paper to hang up on the tree. (*Puts his hand on her head.*) My precious little singing-bird! (*He goes into his room and shuts the door after him.*)

NORA (*after a pause, whispers*): No, no—it isn't true. It's impossible; it must be impossible.

(*The* NURSE *opens the door on the left.*)

NURSE: The little ones are begging so hard to be allowed to come in to mother.

NORA: No, no, no! Don't let them come in to me! You stay with them, Anne.

NURSE: Very well, ma'am. (*Shuts the door.*)

NORA (*pale with terror*): Deprave my little children? Poison my home? (*A short pause. Then she tosses her head.*) It's not true. It can't possibly be true.

ACT II

THE SAME SCENE: *The Christmas-tree is in the corner by the piano, stripped of its ornaments and with burnt-down candle-ends on its dishevelled branches.* NORA's *cloak and hat are lying on the sofa. She is alone in the room, walking about uneasily. She stops by the sofa and takes up her cloak.*

NORA (*drops her cloak*): Someone is coming now! (*Goes to the door and listens.*) No—it's no one. Of course, no one will come today, Christmas Day—nor tomorrow either. But, perhaps—(*Opens the door and looks out.*) No, nothing in the letter-box; its quite empty. (*Comes forward.*) What rubbish! of course he can't be in earnest about it. Such a thing couldn't happen; it is impossible—I have three little children.

(*Enter the* NURSE *from the room on the left, carrying a big cardboard box.*)

NURSE: At last I have found the box with the fancy dress.

NORA: Thanks; put it on the table.

NURSE (*doing so*): But it is very much in need of mending.

NORA: I should like to tear it into a hundred thousand pieces.

NURSE: What an idea! It can easily be put in order—just a little patience.

NORA: Yes, I will go and get Mrs Linde to come and help me with it.

NURSE: What, out again? In this horrible weather? You will catch cold, ma'am, and make yourself ill.

NORA: Well, worse than that might happen. How are the children?

NURSE: The poor little souls are playing with their Christmas presents, but—

NORA: Do they ask much for me?

NURSE: You see, they are so accustomed to have their mother with them.

NORA: Yes, but, nurse, I shall not be able to be so much with them now as I was before.

NURSE: Oh well, young children easily get accustomed to anything.

NORA: Do you think so? Do you think they would forget their mother if she went away altogether?

NURSE: Good heavens!—went away altogether?

NORA: Nurse, I want you to tell me something I have often wondered about—how could you have the heart to put your own child out among strangers?

NURSE: I was obliged to, if I wanted to be little Nora's nurse.

NORA: Yes, but how could you be willing to do it?

NURSE: What, when I was going to get such a good place by it? A poor girl who has got into trouble should be glad to. Besides, that wicked man didn't do a single thing for me.

NORA: But I suppose your daughter has quite forgotten you.

NURSE: No, indeed she hasn't. She wrote to me when she was confirmed, and when she was married.

NORA (*putting her arms round her neck*): Dear old Anne, you were a good mother to me when I was little.

NURSE: Little Nora, poor dear, had no other mother but me.

NORA: And if my little ones had no other mother, I am sure you would—What nonsense I am talking! (*Opens the box.*) Go in to them. Now I must—You will see tomorrow how lovely I shall look.

NURSE: I am sure there will be no one at the ball as lovely as you, ma'am. (*Goes into the room on the left.*)

NORA (*begins to unpack the box, but soon pushes it away from her.*): If only I dared go out. If only no one would come. If only I could be sure nothing would happen here in the meantime. How absurd! No one will come. Only I mustn't think about it. I will brush my muff. What pretty, pretty gloves! Out of my thoughts, out of my thoughts! One, two, three, four, five, six—(*Screams.*)

Oh! there is someone coming—(*Makes a movement towards the door, but stands irresolute.*) (*Enter* MRS LINDE *from the hall, where she has taken off her cloak and hat.*)

NORA: Oh, it's you, Christine. There is no one else out there, is there? How good of you to come!

MRS LINDE: I heard you were up asking for me.

NORA: Yes, I was passing by. As a matter of fact, it is something you could help me with. Let us sit down here on the sofa. Look here. Tomorrow evening there is to be a fancy dress ball at the Stenborgs', who live above us; and Torvald wants me to go as a Neapolitan fisher-girl, and dance the Tarantella that I learnt at Capri.

MRS LINDE: I see; you are going to keep up the character.

NORA: Yes, Torvald wants me to. Look, here is the dress; Torvald had it made for me there, but now it is all so torn, and I haven't any idea—

MRS LINDE: We will easily put that right. It is only some of the trimming come unsewn here and there. Needle and cotton? Now then, that's all we want.

NORA: It *is* nice of you.

MRS LINDE (*sewing*): So you are going to be dressed up tomorrow, Nora. I'll tell you what—I shall come in for a moment and see you in your fine feathers. But I have completely forgotten to thank you for a delightful evening yesterday.

NORA (*gets up, and crosses the stage*): Well, I don't think yesterday was as pleasant as usual. You ought to have come to town a little earlier, Christine. Certainly Torvald does understand how to make a house dainty and attractive.

MRS LINDE: And so do you, it seems to me; you are not your father's daughter for nothing. But tell me, is Doctor Rank always as depressed as he was yesterday?

NORA: No; yesterday it was very noticeable. You see he suffers from a very dangerous disease. He has tuberculosis of the spine, poor creature. His father was a horrible man who committed all sorts of excesses; and that is why his son was sickly from childhood, do you understand?

MRS LINDE (*dropping her sewing*): But, my dearest Nora, how do you know anything about such things?

NORA (*walking about*): Pooh! When you have three children, you get visits now and then from—from married women, who know something of medical matters, and they talk about one thing and another.

MRS LINDE (*goes on sewing. A short silence*): Does Doctor Rank come here every day?

NORA: Every day regularly. He is Torvald's most intimate friend, and a great friend of mine too. He is just like one of the family.

MRS LINDE: But tell me this—is he perfectly sincere? I mean, isn't he the kind of man who is very anxious to make himself agreeable?

NORA: Not in the least. What makes you think that?

MRS LINDE: When you introduced him to me yesterday, he declared he had often heard my name mentioned in this house; but afterwards I noticed that your husband hadn't the slightest idea who I was. So how could Doctor Rank—?

NORA: That's quite right, Christine. Torvald is so absurdly fond of me that he wants me absolutely to himself, as he says. At first he used to seem almost jealous if I mentioned any of the dear folk at home, so naturally I gave up doing so. But I often talk about such things with Doctor Rank; because he likes hearing about them.

MRS LINDE: Listen to me, Nora. You are still very like a child in many things, and I am older than you in many ways and have a little more experience. Let me tell you this—You ought to make an end of it with Doctor Rank.

NORA: What ought I to make an end of?

MRS LINDE: Of two things, I think. Yesterday you talked some nonsense about a rich admirer who was to leave you money—

NORA: An admirer who doesn't exist, unfortunately! But what then?

MRS LINDE: Is Doctor Rank a man of means?

NORA: Yes, he is.

MRS LINDE: And he has no one to provide for?

NORA: No, no one; but—

MRS LINDE: And comes here every day?

NORA: Yes, I told you so.

MRS LINDE: But how can this well-bred man be so tactless?

NORA: I don't understand you at all.

MRS LINDE: Don't prevaricate, Nora. Do you suppose I don't guess who lent you the two hundred and fifty pounds?

NORA: Are you out of your senses? How can you think of such a thing! A friend of ours, who comes here every day! Do you realize what a horribly painful position that would be?

MRS LINDE: Then it really isn't him?

NORA: No, certainly not. It would never have entered my head for a moment. Besides, he had no money to lend then; he came into his money afterwards.

MRS LINDE: Well, I think that was lucky for you, my dear Nora.

NORA: No, it would never have come into my head to ask Doctor Rank. Although I am quite sure that if I had asked him—

MRS LINDE: But of course you won't.

NORA: Of course not. I have no reason to think it could possibly be necessary. But I am quite sure that if I told Doctor Rank—

MRS LINDE: Behind your husband's back?

NORA: I must make an end of it with the other one, and that will be behind his back too. I *must* make an end of it with him.

MRS LINDE: Yes, that is what I told you yesterday, but—

NORA (*walking up and down*): A man can put a thing like that straight much easier than a woman—

MRS LINDE: One's husband, yes.

NORA: Nonsense! (*Standing still.*) When you pay off a debt you get your bond back, don't you?

MRS LINDE: Yes, as a matter of course.

NORA: And can tear it into a hundred thousand pieces, and burn it up—the nasty dirty paper!

MRS LINDE (*looks hard at her, lays down her sewing, and gets up slowly*): Nora, you are concealing something from me.

NORA: Do I look as if I were?

MRS LINDE: Something has happened to you since yesterday morning. Nora, what is it?

NORA (*going nearer to her*): Christine! (*Listens.*) Hush! There's Torvald come home. Do you mind going in to the children for the present? Torvald can't bear to see dress-making going on. Let Anne help you.

MRS LINDE (*gathering some of the things together*): Certainly—but I am not going away from here till we have had it out with one another. (*She goes into the room on the left, as* HELMER *comes in from the hall.*)

NORA (*going up to* HELMER): I have wanted you so much, Torvald dear.

HELMER: Was that the dressmaker?

NORA: No, it was Christine; she is helping me to put my dress in order. You will see I shall look quite smart.

HELMER: Wasn't that a happy thought of mine, now?

NORA: Splendid! But don't you think it is nice of me, too, to do as you wish?

HELMER: Nice?—because you do as your husband wishes? Well, well, you little rogue, I am sure you didn't mean it in that way. But I am not going to disturb you; you will want to be trying on your dress, I expect.

NORA: I suppose you are going to work.

HELMER: Yes. (*Shows her a bundle of papers.*) Look at that. I have just been into the Bank. (*Turns to go into his room.*)

NORA: Torvald.

HELMER: Yes.

NORA: If your little squirrel were to ask you for something very, very prettily—?

HELMER: What then?

NORA: Would you do it?

HELMER: I should like to hear what it is, first.

NORA: Your squirrel would run about and do all her tricks if you would be nice, and do what she wants.

HELMER: Speak plainly.

NORA: Your skylark would chirp about in every room, with her song rising and falling—

HELMER: Well, my skylark does that anyhow.

NORA: I would play the fairy and dance for you in the moonlight, Torvald.

HELMER: Nora—you surely don't mean that request you made to me this morning?

NORA (*going near him*): Yes, Torvald, I beg you so earnestly—

HELMER: Have you really the courage to open up that question again?

NORA: Yes, dear, you *must* do as I ask; you *must* let Krogstad keep his post in the Bank.

HELMER: My dear Nora, it is his post that I have arranged Mrs Linde shall have.

NORA: Yes, you have been awfully kind about that; but you could just as well dismiss some other clerk instead of Krogstad.

HELMER: This is simply incredible obstinacy! Because you chose to give him a thoughtless promise that you would speak for him, I am expected to—

NORA: That isn't the reason, Torvald. It is for your own sake. This fellow writes in the most scurrilous newspapers; you have told me so yourself. He can do you an unspeakable amount of harm. I am frightened to death of him—

HELMER: Ah, I understand; it is recollections of the past that scare you.

NORA: What do you mean?

HELMER: Naturally you are thinking of your father.

NORA: Yes—yes, of course. Remember what these malicious creatures wrote in the papers about father, and how horribly they slandered him. I believe they would have procured his dismissal if the Ministry hadn't sent you over to inquire into it, and if you hadn't been so kindly disposed and helpful to him.

HELMER: My little Nora, there is an important difference between your father and me. Your father's reputation as a public official was not above suspicion. Mine is, and I hope it will continue to be so, as long as I hold my office.

NORA: You never can tell what mischief these men may contrive. We ought to be so well off, so snug and happy here in our peaceful home, and have no cares—you and I and the children, Torvald! That is why I beg you so earnestly—

HELMER: And it is just by interceding for him that you make it impossible for me to keep him. It is already known at the Bank that I mean to dismiss Krogstad. Is it to get about now that the new manager has changed his mind at his wife's bidding—

NORA: And what if it did?

HELMER: Of course!—if only this obstinate little persons can get her way! Do you suppose I am going to make myself ridiculous before my whole staff, to let people think that I am a man to be swayed by all sorts of outside influence? I should very soon feel the consequences of it, I can tell you! And besides, there is one thing that makes it quite impossible for me to have Krogstad in the Bank as long as I am manager.

NORA: Whatever is that?

HELMER: His moral failings I might perhaps have overlooked, if necessary—

NORA: Yes, you could—couldn't you?

HELMER: And I hear he is a good worker, too. But I knew him when we were boys. It was one of those rash friendships that so often prove an embarrassment later. I may as well tell you plainly, we were once on very intimate terms with one another. But this tactless fellow has no restraint when other people are present. On the contrary, he thinks it gives him the right to adopt a familiar tone with me, and every minute it is 'I say, Helmer, old fellow!' and that sort of thing. I assure you it is extremely painful for me.

He would make my position in the Bank intolerable.

NORA: Torvald, I don't believe you mean that.

HELMER: Don't you? Why not?

NORA: Because it is such a narrow-minded way of looking at things.

HELMER: What are you saying? Narrow-minded? Do you think I am narrow-minded?

NORA: No, just the opposite, dear—and it is exactly for that reason.

HELMER: It's the same thing. You say my point of view is narrow-minded, so I must be so too. Narrow-minded! Very well—I must put an end to this. (*Goes to the hall door and calls.*) Helen!

NORA: What are you going to do?

HELMER (*looking among his papers*): Settle it. (*Enter* MAID.) Look here; take this letter and go downstairs with it at once. Find a messenger and tell him to deliver it, and be quick. The address is on it, and here is the money.

MAID: Very well, sir. (*Exit with the letter.*)

HELMER (*putting his papers together*): Now then, little Miss Obstinate.

NORA (*breathlessly*): Torvald—what was that letter?

HELMER: Krogstad's dismissal.

NORA: Call her back, Torvald! There is still time. Oh Torvald, call her back! Do it for my sake—for the children's sake! Do you hear me, Torvald? Call her back! You don't know what that letter can bring upon us.

HELMER: It's too late.

NORA: Yes, it's too late.

HELMER: My dear Nora, I can forgive the anxiety you are in, although really it is an insult to me. It is, indeed. Isn't it an insult to think that I should be afraid of a starving penpusher's vengeance? But I forgive you nevertheless, because it is such eloquent witness to your great love for me. (*Takes her in his arms.*) And that is as it should be, my own darling Nora. Come what will, you may be sure I shall have both courage and strength if they be needed. You will see I am man enough to take everything upon myself.

NORA (*in a horror-stricken voice*): What do you mean by that?

HELMER: Everything, I say—

NORA (*recovering herself*): You will never have to do that.

HELMER: That's right. Well, we will share it, Nora, as man and wife should. That is how it shall be. (*Caressing her.*) Are you content now? There! there!—not these frightened dove's eyes! The whole thing is only the wildest fancy!—.Now, you must go and play through the Tarantella and practise with your tambourine.

I shall go into the inner office and shut the door, and I shall hear nothing; you can make as much noise as you please. (*Turns back at the door.*) And when Rank comes, tell him where he will find me. (*Nods to her, takes his papers and goes into his room, and shuts the door after him.*)

NORA (*bewildered with anxiety, stands as if rooted to the spot, and whispers*): He was capable of doing it. He will do it. Hè will do it in spite of everything—No, not that! Never, never! Anything rather than that! Oh, for some help, some way out of it! (*The doorbell rings.*) Doctor Rank! Anything rather than that—anything, whatever it is! (*She puts her hands over her face, pulls herself together, goes to the door, and opens it.* RANK *is standing outside, hanging up his coat. During the following dialogue it begins to grow dark.*)

NORA: Good afternoon, Doctor Rank. I knew your ring. But you mustn't go in to Torvald now; I think he is busy with something.

RANK: And you?

NORA (*brings him in and shuts the door after him*): Oh, you know very well I always have time for you.

RANK: Thank you. I shall make use of as much of it as I can.

NORA: What do you mean by that? As much of it as you can?

RANK: Well, does that alarm you?

NORA: It was such a strange way of putting it. Is anything likely to happen?

RANK: Nothing but what I have long been prepared for. But I certainly didn't expect it to happen so soon.

NORA (*gripping him by the arm*): What have you found out? Doctor Rank, you must tell me.

RANK (*sitting down by the stove*): It is all up with me. And it can't be helped.

NORA (*with a sigh of relief*): Is it about yourself?

RANK: Who else? It is no use lying to one's self. I am the most wretched of all my patients, Mrs Helmer. Lately I have been taking stock of my internal economy. Bankrupt! Probably within a month I shall lie rotting in the churchyard.

NORA: What an ugly thing to say!

RANK: The thing itself is cursedly ugly, and the worst of it is that I shall have to face so much more that is ugly before that. I shall only make one more examination of myself; when I have done that, I shall know pretty certainly when it will be that the horrors of dissolution will begin. There is something I want to tell you. Helmer's refined nature gives him an unconquerable disgust at everything that is ugly; I won't have him in my sickroom.

NORA: Oh, but, Doctor Rank—

RANK: I won't have him there. Not on any account. I bar my door to him. As soon as I am quite certain that the worst has come, I shall send you my card with a black cross on it, and then you will know that the loathsome end has begun.

NORA: You are quite absurd today. And I wanted you so much to be in a really good humour.

RANK: With death stalking beside me?—To have to pay this penalty for another man's sin! Is there any justice in that? And in every single family, in one way or another, some such inexorable retribution is being exacted—

NORA (*putting her hands over her ears*): Rubbish! Do talk about something cheerful.

RANK: Oh, it's a mere laughing matter, the whole thing. My poor innocent spine has to suffer for my father's youthful amusements.

NORA (*sitting at the table on the left*): I suppose you mean that he was too partial to asparagus and pâté de foie gras, don't you?

RANK: Yes, and to truffles.

NORA: Truffles, yes. And oysters too, I suppose?

RANK: Oysters, of course, that goes without saying.

NORA: And heaps of port and champagne. It is sad that all these nice things should take their revenge on our bones.

RANK: Especially that they should revenge themselves on the unlucky bones of those who have not had the satisfaction of enjoying them.

NORA: Yes, that's the saddest part of it all.

RANK (*with a searching look at her*): Hm!—

NORA (*after a short pause*): Why did you smile?

RANK: No, it was you that laughed.

NORA: No, it was you that smiled, Doctor Rank!

RANK (*rising*): You are a greater rascal than I thought.

NORA: I am in a silly mood today.

RANK: So it seems.

NORA (*putting her hands on his shoulders*): Dear, dear Doctor Rank, death mustn't take you away from Torvald and me.

RANK: It is a loss you would easily recover from. Those who are gone are soon forgotten.

NORA (*looking at him anxiously*): Do you believe that?

RANK: People form new ties, and then—

NORA: Who will form new ties?

RANK: Both you and Helmer, when I am gone. You yourself are already on the high road to it, I think. What did that Mrs Linde want here last night?

NORA: Oho!—you don't mean to say you are jealous of poor Christine?

RANK: Yes, I am. She will be my successor in this house. When I am done for, this woman will—

NORA: Hush! don't speak so loud. She is in that room.

RANK: Today again. There, you see.

NORA: She has only come to sew my dress for me. Good gracious, how unreasonable you are! (*Sits down on the sofa.*) Be nice now, Doctor Rank, and tomorrow you'll see how beautifully I shall dance, and you can imagine I am doing it all for you—and for Torvald too, of course. (*Takes various things out of the box.*) Doctor Rank, come and sit down here, and I will show you something.

RANK (*sitting down*): What is it?

NORA: Just look at those!

RANK: Silk stockings.

NORA: Flesh-coloured. Aren't they lovely? It is so dark here now, but tomorrow—No, no, no! you must only look at the feet. Oh well, you may have permission to look at the legs too.

RANK: Hm!—

NORA: Why are you looking so critical? Don't you think they will fit me?

RANK: I have no means of forming an opinion about that.

NORA (*looks at him for a moment*): Shame on you! (*Hits him lightly on the ear with the stockings.*) That's to punish you. (*Folds them up again.*)

RANK: And what other nice things am I to be allowed to see?

NORA: Not a single thing more, for being so naughty. (*She looks among the things, humming to herself.*)

RANK (*after a short silence*): When I am sitting here, talking to you as intimately as this, I cannot imagine for a moment what would have become of me if I had never come into this house.

NORA (*smiling*): I believe you do feel thoroughly at home with us.

RANK (*in a lower voice, looking straight in front of him*): And to have to leave it all—

NORA: Nonsense, you are not going to leave it.

RANK (*as before*): And not be able to leave behind one the slightest token of one's gratitude, barely a fleeting regret even—nothing but an empty place which the first comer can fill as well as any other.

NORA: And if I asked you now for a—? No!

RANK: For what?

NORA: For a big proof of your friendship—

RANK: Yes, yes!

NORA: I mean a tremendously big favour—

RANK: Would you really make me so happy for once?

NORA: Ah, but you don't know what it is yet.

RANK: No—but tell me.

NORA: I really can't, Doctor Rank. It is something out of all reason; it means advice, and help, and a favour—

RANK: The bigger a thing it is the better I can't conceive what it is you mean. Do tell me. Haven't I your confidence?

NORA: More than anyone else. I know you are my truest and best friend, and so I will tell you what it is. Well, Doctor Rank, it is something you must help me to prevent. You know how devotedly, how inexpressibly deeply Torvald loves me; he would never for a moment hesitate to give his life for me.

RANK (*leaning towards her*): Nora—do you think he is the only one—?

NORA (*with a slight start*): The only one—?

RANK: The only one who would gladly give his life for your sake.

NORA (*sadly*): Is that it?

RANK: I was determined you should know it before I went away, and there will never be a better opportunity than this. Now you know it, Nora. And now you know, too, that you can trust me as you would trust no one else.

NORA (*rises, deliberately and quietly*): Let me pass.

RANK (*makes room for her to pass him, but sits still*): Nora!

NORA (*at the hall door*): Helen, bring in the lamp. (*Goes over to the stove.*) Dear Doctor Rank, that was really horrid of you.

RANK: To have loved you as much as anyone else does? Was that horrid?

NORA: No, but to go and tell me so. There was really no need—

RANK: What do you mean? Did you know—? (MAID *enters with lamp, puts it down on the table, and goes out.*) Nora—Mrs Helmer—tell me, had you any idea of this?

NORA: Oh, how do I know whether I had or whether I hadn't? I really can't tell you—To think you could be so clumsy, Doctor Rank! We were getting on so nicely.

RANK: Well, at all events you know now that you can command me, body and soul. So won't you speak out?

NORA (*looking at him*): After what happened?

RANK: I beg you to let me know what it is.

NORA: I can't tell you anything now.

RANK: Yes, yes. You mustn't punish me in that way. Let me have permission to do for you whatever a man may do.

NORA: You can do nothing for me now. Besides, I really don't need any help at all. You will find that the whole thing is merely fancy on my part. It really is so—of course it is! (*Sits down in the rocking-chair, and looks at him with a smile.*) You are a nice sort of man, Doctor Rank!—don't you feel ashamed of yourself, now the lamp has come?

RANK: Not a bit. But perhaps I had better go—for ever?

NORA: No, indeed, you shall not. Of course you must come here just as before. You know very well Torvald can't do without you.

RANK: Yes, but you?

NORA: Oh, I am always tremendously pleased when you come.

RANK: It is just that, that put me on the wrong track. You are a riddle to me. I have often thought that you would almost as soon be in my company as in Helmer's.

NORA: Yes—you see there are some people one loves best, and others whom one would almost always rather have as companions.

RANK: Yes, there is something in that.

NORA: When I was at home, of course I loved father best. But I always thought it tremendous fun if I could steal down into the maids' room, because they never moralized at all, and talked to each other about such entertaining things.

RANK: I see—it is *their* place I have taken.

NORA (*jumping up and going to him*): Oh, dear, nice Doctor Rank, I never meant that at all. But surely you can understand that being with Torvald is a little like being with father—(*Enter* MAID *from the hall.*)

MAID: If you please, ma'am. (*Whispers and hands her a card.*)

NORA (*glancing at the card*): Oh! (*Puts it in her pocket.*)

RANK: Is there anything wrong?

NORA: No, no, not in the least. It is only something—it is my new dress—

RANK: What? Your dress is lying there.

NORA: Oh, yes, that one; but this is another. I ordered it. Torvald mustn't know about it—

RANK: Oh! Then that was the great secret.

NORA: Of course. Do go in to him; he is sitting in the inner room. Keep him as long as—

RANK: Don't worry; I won't let him escape. (*Goes into* HELMER's room.)

NORA (*to the* MAID): And he is standing waiting in the kitchen?

MAID: Yes; he came up the back stairs.

NORA: But didn't you tell him no one was in?

MAID: Yes, but it was no good.

NORA: He won't go away?

MAID: No: he says he won't until he has seen you, ma'am.

NORA: Well, let him come in—but quietly. Helen, you mustn't say anything about it to anyone. It is a surprise for my husband.

MAID: Yes, ma'am, I quite understand. (*Exit.*)

NORA: This dreadful thing is going to happen! It will happen in spite of me! No, no, no, it can't happen—it shan't happen! (*She bolts the door of* HELMER'*s room. The* MAID *opens the hall door for* KROGSTAD *and shuts it after him. He is wearing a fur coat, high boots, and a fur cap.*)

NORA (*advancing towards him*): Speak quietly—my husband is at home.

KROGSTAD: I don't care about that.

NORA: What do you want of me?

KROGSTAD: An explanation of something.

NORA: Hurry up then. What is it?

KROGSTAD: You know, I suppose, that I have got my dismissal.

NORA: I couldn't prevent it, Mr Krogstad. I fought as hard as I could on your side, but it was no good.

KROGSTAD: Does your husband love you so little, then? He knows what I can expose you to, and yet he ventures—

NORA: How can you suppose that he has any knowledge of the sort?

KROGSTAD: I didn't suppose so at all. It would not be the least like our dear Torvald Helmer to show so much courage—

NORA: Mr Krogstad, a little respect for my husband, please.

KROGSTAD: Certainly—all the respect he deserves. But since you have kept the matter so carefully to yourself, I can only suppose that you have a little clearer idea, than you had yesterday, of what it actually is that you have done?

NORA: More than you could ever teach me.

KROGSTAD: Yes, such a bad lawyer as I am.

NORA: What is it you want of me?

KROGSTAD: Only to see how you were, Mrs Helmer. I have been thinking about you all day long. A mere cashier, a penpusher, a—well, a man like me—even he has a little of what is called feeling, you know.

NORA: Show it, then; think of my little children.

KROGSTAD: Have you and your husband thought of mine? But never mind about that, I only wanted to tell you that you need not take this matter too seriously. In the first place there will be no accusation made on my part.

NORA: No, of course not; I was sure of that.

KROGSTAD: The whole thing can be arranged amicably; there is no reason why anyone should know anything about it. It will remain a secret between us three.

NORA: My husband must never get to know anything about it.

KROGSTAD: How will you be able to prevent it? Am I to understand that you can pay the balance that is owing?

NORA: No, not just at present.

KROGSTAD: Or perhaps that you have some expedient for raising the money soon?

NORA: No expedient that I mean to make use of.

KROGSTAD: Well, in any case, it would have been of no use to you now. If you stood there with ever so much money in your hand, I would never part with your bond.

NORA: Tell me what purpose you mean to put it to.

KROGSTAD: I shall only preserve it—keep it in my possession. No one who is not concerned in the matter shall have the slightest hint of it. So that if the thought of it has driven you to any desperate resolution—

NORA: It has.

KROGSTAD: If you had it in your mind to run away from your home—

NORA: I had.

KROGSTAD: Or even something worse—

NORA: How could you know that?

KROGSTAD: Give up the idea.

NORA: How did you know I had thought of *that*?

KROGSTAD: Most of us think of that at first. I did, too—but I hadn't the courage.

NORA (*faintly*): Nor had I.

KROGSTAD (*in a tone of relief*): No, that's it, isn't it—you hadn't the courage either?

NORA: No, I haven't—I haven't.

KROGSTAD: Besides, it would have been a very foolish thing. Once the first storm at home is over—I have a letter for your husband in my pocket.

NORA: Telling him everything?

KROGSTAD: In as lenient a manner as I possibly could.

NORA (*quickly*): He mustn't get the letter. Tear it up. I'll find some means of getting money.

KROGSTAD: Excuse me, Mrs Helmer, but I think I told you just now—

NORA: I am not speaking of what I owe you. Tell me what sum you are asking my husband for, and I will get the money.

KROGSTAD: I am not asking your husband for a penny.

NORA: What do you want, then?

KROGSTAD: I will tell you, I want to rehabilitate myself, Mrs Helmer; I want to get on; and in that your husband must help me. For the last year and a half I have not had a hand in anything dishonourable, and all that time I have been struggling in most restricted circumstances. I was content to work my way up step by step. Now I am turned out, and I am not going to be satisfied with merely being taken into favour again. I want to get on, I tell you. I want to get into the Bank again, in a higher position. Your husband must make a place for me—

NORA: That he will never do!

KROGSTAD: He will; I know him; he dare not protest. And as soon as I am in there again with him, then you will see! Within a year I shall be the manager's right hand. It will be Nils Krogstad and not Torvald Helmer who manages the Bank.

NORA: That's a thing you will never see!

KROGSTAD: Do you mean that you will—?

NORA: I have courage enough for it now.

KROGSTAD: Oh, you can't frighten me. A fine, spoilt woman like you—

NORA: You will see, you will see.

KROGSTAD: Under the ice, perhaps? Down into the cold, coal-black water? And then, in the spring, to float up to the surface, all horrible and unrecognizable, with your hair fallen out—

NORA: You can't frighten me.

KROGSTAD: Nor you me. People don't do such things, Mrs Helmer. Besides, what use would it be? I should have him completely in my power all the same.

NORA: Afterwards? When I am no longer—

KROGSTAD: Have you forgotten that it is I who have the keeping of your reputation? (NORA *stands speechlessly looking at him.*) Well, now, I have warned you. Don't do anything foolish. When Helmer has had my letter; I shall expect a message from him. And be sure you remember that it is your husband himself who has forced me into such ways as this again. I will never forgive him for that. Good-bye, Mrs Helmer. (*Exit through the hall.*)

NORA (*goes to the hall door, opens it slightly, and listens*): He is going. He is not putting the letter in the box. Oh no, no! that's impossible! (*Opens the door by degrees.*) What is that? He is standing outside. He is not going downstairs. Is he hesitating? Can he—? (*A letter drops into the box; then* KROGSTAD*'s footsteps are heard, till they die away as he goes downstairs,* NORA *utters a stifled cry, and runs across the room to the table by the sofa. A short pause.*)

NORA: In the letter-box. (*Steals across to the hall door.*) It's lying there—Torvald, Torvald, there is no hope for us now! (MRS LINDE *comes in from the room on the left, carrying the dress.*)

MRS LINDE: There, I can't see anything more to mend now. Would you like to try it on—?

NORA (*in a hoarse whisper*): Christine, come here.

MRS LINDE (*throwing the dress down on the sofa*): What is the matter with you? You look so agitated!

NORA: Come here. Do you see that letter? There, look—You can see it through the glass in the letter-box.

MRS LINDE: Yes, I see it.

NORA: That letter is from Krogstad.

MRS LINDE: Nora—it was Krogstad who lent you the money!

NORA: Yes, and now Torvald will know all about it.

MRS LINDE: Believe me, Nora, that's the best thing for both of you.

NORA: You don't know all. I forged a name.

MRS LINDE: Good heavens—!

NORA: I only want to say this to you, Christine—you must be my witness.

MRS LINDE: Your witness? What do you mean ? What am I to—?

NORA: If I should go out of my mind—and it might easily happen—

MRS LINDE: Nora!

NORA: Or if anything else should happen to me—anything, for instance, that might prevent my being here—

MRS LINDE: Nora! Nora! you are quite out of your mind.

NORA: And if it should happen that there were someone who wanted to take all the responsibility, all the blame, you understand—

MRS LINDE: Yes, yes—but how can you suppose—?

NORA: Then you must be my witness, that it is not true, Christine. I am not out of my mind at all; I am in my right senses now, and I tell you no one else has known anything about it; I, and I alone, did the whole thing. Remember that.

MRS LINDE: I will, indeed. But I don't understand all this.

NORA: How should you understand it? A wonderful thing is going to happen!

MRS LINDE: A wonderful thing?

NORA: Yes, a wonderful thing!—But it is so terrible, Christine; it *mustn't* happen, not for all the world.

MRS LINDE: I will go at once and see Krogstad.

NORA: Don't go to him; he will do you some harm.

MRS LINDE: There was a time when he would gladly do anything for my sake.

NORA: He?

MRS LINDE: Where does he live?

NORA: How should I know—? (*feeling in her pocket*), here is his card. But the letter, the letter—!

HELMER (*calls from his room, knocking at the door*): Nora!

NORA (*cries out anxiously*): Oh, what's that? What do you want?

HELMER: Don't be so frightened. We are not coming in: you have locked the door. Are you trying on your dress?

NORA: Yes, that's it. I look so nice, Torvald.

MRS LINDE (*who has read the card*): I see he lives at the corner here.

NORA: Yes, but it's no use. It is hopeless. The letter is lying there in the box.

MRS LINDE: And your husband keeps the key?

NORA: Yes, always.

MRS LINDE: Krogstad must ask for his letter back unread, he must find some excuse—

NORA: But it is just at this time that Torvald generally—

MRS LINDE: You must delay him. Go in to him in the meantime. I'll come back as soon as I can. (*She goes out hurriedly through the hall door.*)

NORA (*goes to HELMER's door, opens it, and beeps in*): Torvald!

HELMER (*from the inner room*): Well ? May I venture at last to come into my own room again? Come along, Rank, now you will see—(*Halting in the doorway.*) But what is this?

NORA: What is what, dear?

HELMER: Rank led me to expect a splendid transformation.

RANK (*in the doorway*): I understood so, but evidently I was mistaken.

NORA: Yes, nobody is to have the chance of admiring me in my dress until tomorrow.

HELMER: But, my dear Nora you look so worn out. Have you been practising too much?

NORA: No, I have not practised at all.

HELMER: But you will need to—

NORA: Yes, indeed I shall, Torvald. But I can't get on a bit without you to help me. I have absolutely forgotten the whole thing.

HELMER: Oh, we will soon work it up again.

NORA: Yes, help me, Torvald. Promise that you will! I am so nervous about it—all the people—You must give yourself up to me entirely this evening. Not the tiniest bit of business—you mustn't even take a pen in your hand. Will you promise, Torvald dear?

HELMER: I promise. This evening I will be wholly and absolutely at your service, you helpless little mortal. Ah, by the way, first of all I will just—(*Goes towards the hall door.*)

NORA: What are you going to do there?

HELMER: Only to see if any letters have come.

NORA: No, no! don't do that, Torvald!

HELMER: Why not?

NORA: Torvald, please don't. There is nothing there.

HELMER: Well, let me look. (*Turns to go to the letter-box.* NORA, *at the piano, plays the first bars of the Tarantella.* HELMER *stops in the doorway.*) Aha!

NORA: I can't dance tomorrow if I don't practise with you.

HELMER (*going up to her*): Are you really so afraid of it, dear?

NORA: Yes, so dreadfully afraid of it. Let me practise at once; there is time now, before we go to dinner. Sit down and play for me, Torvald dear; criticize me, and correct me as you play.

HELMER: With great pleasure, if you wish me to. (*Sits down at the piano.*)

NORA (*takes out of the box a tambourine and a long variegated shawl. She hastily drapes the shawl round her. Then she springs to the front of the stage and calls out*): Now play for me! I am going to dance!

(HELMER *plays and* NORA *dances,* RANK *stands by the piano behind* HELMER, *and looks on.*)

HELMER (*as he plays*): Slower, slower!

NORA: I can't do it any other way.

HELMER: Not so violently, Nora!

NORA: This is the way.

HELMER (*stops playing*): No, no—that is not a bit right.

NORA (*laughing and swinging the tambourine*): Didn't I tell you so?

RANK: Let me play for her.

HELMER (*getting up*): Yes, do. I can correct her better then. (RANK *sits down at the piano and plays,* NORA *dances more and more wildly,* HELMER *has taken up a position beside the stove, and during her dance gives her frequent instructions. She does not seem to hear him; her hair comes down and falls over her shoulders; she pays no attention to it, but goes on dancing. Enter* MRS LINDE.)

MRS LINDE (*standing as if spell-bound in the doorway*): Oh!—

NORA (*as she dances*): Such fun, Christine!

HELMER: My dear darling Nora, you are dancing as if your life depended on it.

NORA: So it does.

HELMER: Stop, Rank; this is sheer madness. Stop, I tell you! (RANK *stops playing, and* NORA *suddenly stands still.* HELMER *goes up to her.*) I could never have believed it. You have forgotten everything I taught you.

NORA (*throwing away the tambourine*): There, you see.

HELMER: You will want a lot of coaching.

NORA: Yes, you see how much I need it. You must coach me up to the last minute. Promise me that, Torvald!

HELMER: You can depend on me.

NORA: You must not think of anything but me, either today or tomorrow; you mustn't open a single letter—not even open the letter-box—

HELMER: Ah, you are still afraid of that fellow—

NORA: Yes, indeed I am.

HELMER: Nora, I can tell from your looks that there is a letter from him lying there.

NORA: I don't know; I think there is; but you mustn't read anything of that kind now. Nothing horrid must come between us till this is all over.

RANK (*whispers to* HELMER): You mustn't contradict her.

HELMER (*taking her in his arms*): The child shall have her way. But tomorrow night, after you have danced—

NORA: Then you will be free. (*The* MAID *appears in the doorway to the right.*)

MAID: Dinner is served, ma'am.

NORA: We will have champagne, Helen.

MAID: Very good, ma'am. *Exit.*

HELMER: Hallo!—are we going to have a banquet?

NORA: Yes, a champagne banquet till the small hours. (*Calls out.*) And a few macaroons, Helen—lots, just for once!

HELMER: Come, come, don't be so wilde and nervous. Be my own little skylark, as you used.

NORA: Yes, dear, I will. But go in now, and you too, Doctor Rank. Christine, you must help me to do up my hair.

RANK (*whispers to* HELMER *as they go out*): I suppose there is nothing—she is not expecting anything?

HELMER: Far from it, my dear fellow; it is simply nothing more than this childish nervousness I was telling you of. (*They go into the right-hand room.*)

NORA: Well!

MRS LINDE: Gone out of town.

NORA: I could tell from your face.

MRS LINDE: He is corning home tomorrow evening. I wrote a note for him.

NORA: You should have let it alone; you must prevent nothing. After all, it is splendid to be waiting for a wonderful thing to happen.

MRS LINDE: What is it that you are waiting for?

NORA: Oh, you wouldn't understand. Go in to them, I will come in a moment, (MRS LINDE *goes into the dining-room,* NORA *stands still for a little while, as if to compose herself. Then she looks at her watch.*) Five o'clock. Seven hours till midnight; and then twenty-four hours till the next midnight. Then the Tarantella will be over. Twenty-four and seven? Thirty-one hours to live.

HELMER (*from the doorway on the right*): Where's my little skylark?

NORA (*going to him with her arms outstretched*): Here she is!

ACT III

THE SAME SCENE: *The table has been placed in the middle of the stage, with chairs round it. A lamp is burning on the table. The door into the hall stands open. Dance music is heard in the room above,* MRS LINDE *is sitting at the table idly turning over the leaves of a book; she tries to read, but does not seem able to collect her thoughts. Every now and then she listens intently for a sound at the outer door.*

MRS LINDE (*looking at her watch*): Not yet—and the time is nearly up. If only he does not—(*Listens again.*) Ah, there he is. (*Goes into the hall and opens the outer door carefully. Light footsteps are heard on the stairs. She whispers.*) Come in. There is no one here.

KROGSTAD (*in the doorway*): I found a note from you at home. What does this mean?

MRS LINDE: It is absolutely necessary that I should have a talk with you.

KROGSTAD: Really? And is it absolutely necessary that it should be here?

MRS LINDE: It is impossible where I live; there is no private entrance to my rooms. Come in; we are quite alone. The maid is asleep, and the Helmers are at the dance upstairs.

KROGSTAD (*coming into the room*): Are the Helmers really at a dance tonight?

MRS LINDE: Yes, why not?

KROGSTAD: Certainly—why not?

MRS LINDE: Now, Nils, let us have a talk.

KROGSTAD: Can we two have anything to talk about?

MRS LINDE: We have a great deal to talk about.

KROGSTAD: I shouldn't have thought so.

MRS LINDE: No, you have never properly understood me.

KROGSTAD: Was there anything else to understand except what was obvious to all the world—a heartless woman jilts a man when a more lucrative chance turns up?

MRS LINDE: Do you believe I am as absolutely heartless as all that? And do you believe that I did it with a light heart?

KROGSTAD: Didn't you?

MRS LINDE: Nils, did you really think that?

KROGSTAD: If it were as you say, why did you write to me as you did at the time?

MRS LINDE: I could do nothing else. As I had to break with you, it was my duty also to put an end to all that you felt for me.

KROGSTAD (*wringing his hands*): So that was it. And all this—only for the sake of money!

MRS LINDE: You mustn't forget that I had a helpless mother and two little brothers. We couldn't wait for you, Nils; your prospects seemed hopeless then.

KROGSTAD: That may be so, but you had no right to throw me over for anyone else's sake.

MRS LINDE: I really don't know. Often I used to ask myself if I had the right to do it.

KROGSTAD (*more gently*): When I lost you, it was as if all the solid ground went from under my feet. Look at me now—I am a shipwrecked man clinging to a bit of wreckage.

MRS LINDE: But help may be near.

KROGSTAD: It *was* near; but then you came and stood in my way.

MRS LINDE: Unintentionally, Nils. It was only today that I learnt it was your place I was going to take in the Bank.

KROGSTAD: I believe you, if you say so. But now that you know it, are you not going to give it up to me?

MRS LINDE: No, because that wouldn't benefit you in the least.

KROGSTAD: Oh, benefit, benefit—I would have done it, benefit or not.

MRS LINDE: I have learnt to act prudently. Life, and hard, bitter necessity have taught me that.

KROGSTAD: And life has taught me not to believe in fine speeches.

MRS LINDE: Then life has taught you something very sensible. But deeds you must believe in?

KROGSTAD: What do you mean by that?

MRS LINDE: You said you were like a shipwrecked man clinging to some wreckage.

KROGSTAD: I had good reason to say so.

MRS LINDE: Well, I am like a shipwrecked woman clinging to some wreckage—no one to mourn for, no one to care for.

KROGSTAD: It was your own choice.

MRS LINDE: There was no other choice—then.

KROGSTAD: Well, what now?

MRS LINDE: Nils, how would it be if we two shipwrecked people could join forces?

KROGSTAD: What are you saying?

MRS LINDE: Two on the same piece of wreckage would stand a better chance than each on their own.

KROGSTAD: Christine!

MRS LINDE: What do you suppose brought me to town?

KROGSTAD: Do you mean that you gave me a thought?

MRS LINDE: I could not endure life without work. All my life, as long as I can remember, I have worked, and it has been my greatest and only pleasure. But now I am quite alone in the world—my life is so dreadfully empty and I feel so forsaken. There is not the least pleasure in working for one's self. Nils, give me someone and something to work for.

KROGSTAD: I don't trust that. It is nothing but a woman's overstrained sense of generosity that prompts you to make such an offer of yourself.

MRS LINDE: Have you ever noticed anything of the sort in me?

KROGSTAD: Could you really do it? Tell me—do you know all about my past life?

MRS LINDE: Yes.

KROGSTAD: And do you know what they think of me here?

MRS LINDE: You seemed to me to imply that with me you might have been quite another man.

KROGSTAD: I am certain of it.

MRS LINDE: Is it too late now?

KROGSTAD: Christine, are you saying this deliberately? Yes, I am sure you are. I see it in your face. Have you really the courage, then—?

MRS LINDE: I want to be a mother to someone, and your children need a mother. We two need each other. Nils, I have faith in your real character—I can dare anything together with you.

KROGSTAD (*grasps her hands*): Thanks, thanks, Christine! Now I shall find a way to clear myself in the eyes of the world. Ah, but I forgot—

MRS LINDE (*listening*): Hush! The Tarantella! Go, go!

KROGSTAD: Why? What is it?

MRS LINDE: Do you hear them up there? When that is over, we can expect them back.

KROGSTAD: Yes, yes—I'll go. But it's all no use. Of course you don't know what steps I have taken in the matter of the Helmers.

MRS LINDE: Yes, I know all about that.

KROGSTAD: And in spite of that have you the courage to—?

MRS LINDE: I understand very well to what lengths a man like you might be driven by despair.

KROGSTAD: If I could only undo what I have done!

MRS LINDE: You cannot. Your letter is lying in the letter-box now.

KROGSTAD: Are you sure of that?

MRS LINDE: Quite sure, but—

KROGSTAD (*with a searching look at her*): Is that what it all means?—that you want to save your friend at any cost? Tell me frankly. Is that it?

MRS LINDE: Nils, a woman who has once sold herself for another's sake, doesn't do it a second time.

KROGSTAD: I will ask for my letter back.

MRS LINDE: No, no.

KROGSTAD: Yes, of course I will. I will wait here till Helmer comes; I will tell him he must give me my letter back—that it only concerns my dismissal—that he is not to read it—

MRS LINDE: No, Nils, you must not recall your letter.

KROGSTAD: But tell me, wasn't it for that very purpose that you asked me to meet you here?

MRS LINDE: In my first moment of fright, it was. But twenty-four hours have passed since then, and in that time I have witnessed incredible things in this house. Helmer must know all about it. This unhappy secret must be disclosed; they must have a complete understanding between them, which is impossible with all this concealment and falsehood going on.

KROGSTAD: All right, if you will take the responsibility. But there is one thing I can do in my case, and I shall do it at once.

MRS LINDE (*listening*): You must be quick and go! The dance is over; we aren't safe a moment longer.

KROGSTAD: I'll wait for you below.

MRS LINDE: Yes, do. You must see me back to my door.

KROGSTAD: I have never had such an amazing piece of good fortune in my life! (*Goes out through the outer door. The door between the room and the hall remains open.*)

MRS LINDE (*tidying up the room and laying her hat and cloak ready*): What a difference! What a difference! Someone to work for and live for—a home to bring comfort into. That I will do, indeed. I wish they would be quick and come—(*Listens.*) Ah, there they are now. I must put on my things. (*Takes up her hat and cloak.* HELMER'S *and* NORA'S *voices are heard outside; a key is turned, and* HELMER *brings* NORA *almost by force into the hall. She is in an Italian costume with a large black shawl round her; he is in evening dress, and a black domino which is flying open.*)

NORA (*hanging back in the doorway, and struggling with him*): No, no, no!—don't want to leave so early.

HELMER: But, my dearest Nora—

NORA: Please, Torvald dear—please, *please*—only an hour more.

HELMER: Not a single minute, my sweet Nora. You know that was our agreement. Come along into the room; you are catching cold standing there. (*Hebrings her gently into the room, in spite of her resistance.*)

MRS LINDE: Good evening.

NORA: Christine!

HELMER: You here, so late, Mrs Linde?

MRS LINDE: Yes, you must forgive me; I was so anxious to see Nora in her dress.

NORA: Have you been sitting here waiting for me?

MRS LINDE: Yes, unfortunately I came too late, you had already gone upstairs; and I thought I couldn't go away again without having seen you.

HELMER (*taking off* NORA'S *shawl*): Yes, take a good look at her. I think she is worth looking at. Isn't she charming, Mrs Linde?

MRS LINDE: Yes, indeed she is.

HELMER: Doesn't she look remarkably pretty? Everyone thought so at the dance. But she is terribly self-willed, this sweet little person. What are we to do with her? You'll hardly believe that I almost had to bring her away by force.

NORA: Torvald, you will repent not having let me stay, even if it were only for half an hour.

HELMER: Listen to her, Mrs Linde! She had danced her Tarantella, and it had been a tremendous success, as it deserved—although possibly the performance was a trifle too realistic—a little more so, I mean, than was strictly compatible with the limitations of art. But never mind about that! The chief thing is, she had made a success—she had made a tremendous success. Do you think I was going to let her remain there after that, and spoil the effect? No, indeed! I took my charming little Capri maiden, I should say—on my arm; took one quick turn round the room; a curtsy on either side, and, as they say in novels, the beautiful apparition disappeared. An exit ought always to be effective, Mrs Linde; but that is what I cannot make Nora understand. Pooh! this room is hot. (*Throws his comino on a chair, and opens the door of his room.*) Hallo! it's all dark in here. Oh, of course—excuse me— (*He goes in, and lights some candles.*)

NORA (*in a hurried and breathless whisper*): Well?

MRS LINDE (*in a low voice*): I have had a talk with him.

NORA: Yes, and—

MRS LINDE: Nora, you must tell your husband all about it.

NORA (*in an expressionless voice*): I knew it.

MRS LINDE: You have nothing to be afraid of as far as Krogstad is concerned; but you must tell him.

NORA: I won't tell him.

MRS LINDE: Then the letter will.

NORA: Thank you, Christine. Now I know what I must do. Hush—!

HELMER (*coming in again*): Well, Mrs Linde, have you admired her?

MRS LINDE: Yes, and now I will say good night.

HELMER: What, already? Is this yours, this knitting?

MRS LINDE (*taking it*): Yes, thank you, I had very nearly forgotten it.

HELMER: So you knit?

MRS LINDE: Of course.

HELMER: Do you know, you ought to embroider.

MRS LINDE: Really? Why?

HELMER: Yes, it's far more becoming. Let me show you. You hold the embroidery thus in your left hand, and use the needle with the right—like this—with a long, easy sweep Do you see?

MRS LINDE: Yes, perhaps—

HELMER: But in the case of knitting—that can never be anything but ungraceful; look here—the arms close together, the knitting-needles going up and down—it has a sort of Chinese effect— That was really excellent champagne they gave us.

MRS LINDE: Well—good night, Nora, and don't be self-willed any more.

HELMER: That's right, Mrs. Linde.

MRS LINDE: Good night, Mr. Helmer.

HELMER (*accompanying her to the door*): Good night, good night. I hope you will get home all right. I should be very happy to—but you haven't any great distance to go. Good night, good night. (*She goes out; he shuts the door after her, and comes in again.*) Ah!—at last we have got rid of her. She is a frightful bore, that woman.

NORA: Aren't you very tired, Torvald?

HELMER: No, not in the least.

NORA: Nor sleepy?

HELMER: Not a bit. On the contrary, I feel extraordinarily lively. And you?—you really look both tired and sleepy.

NORA: Yes, I am very tired. I want to go to sleep at once.

HELMER: There, you see it was quite right of me not to let you stay there any longer.

NORA: Everything you do is quite right, Torvald.

HELMER (*kissing her on the forehead*): Now my little skylark is speaking reasonably. Did you notice what good spirits Rank was in this evening?

NORA: Really? Was he? I didn't speak to him at all.

HELMER: And I very little, but I haven't for a long time seen him in such good form. (*Looks for a while at her and then goes nearer to her.*) It is wonderful to be at home by ourselves again, to be all alone with you—you fascinating, charming little darling!

NORA: Don't look at me like that, Torvald.

HELMER: Why shouldn't I look at my dearest treasure?—at all the beauty that is mine, all my very own?

NORA (*going to the other side of the table*): You mustn't say things like that to me tonight.

HELMER (*following her*): You have still got the Tarantella in your blood, I see. And it makes you more captivating than ever. Listen—the guests are beginning to go now. (*In a lower voice.*) Nora—soon the whole house will be quiet.

NORA: Yes, I hope so.

HELMER: Yes, my own darling Nora. Do you know, when I am out at a party with you like this why I speak so little to you, why I keep away from you, and only send a stolen glance in your direction now and then?—do you know why I do that? It is because I make believe to myself that we are secretly in love, and you are my secretly promised bride, and that no one suspects there is anything between us.

NORA: Yes, yes—I know quite well your thoughts are with me all the time.

HELMER: And when we are leaving, and I am putting the shawl over your beautiful young shoulders—on your lovely neck—then I imagine that you are my young bride and that we have just come from the wedding, and I am bringing you for the first time into our home—to be alone with you for the first time—quite alone with my shy little darling! All this evening I have longed for nothing but you. When I watched the seductive figures of the Tarantella, my blood was on fire; I could endure it no longer, and that was why I brought you down so early—

NORA: Go away, Torvald! You must let me go. I won't—

HELMER: What's that? You're joking, my little Nora! You won't—you won't? Am I not your husband—? (*A knock is heard at the outer door.*)

NORA (*starting*): Did you hear—?

HELMER (*going into the hall*): Who is it?

RANK (*outside*): It's me. May I come in for a moment?

HELMER (*in a fretful whisper*): Oh, what does he want now? (*Aloud.*) Wait a minute! (*Unlocks the door.*) Well, that's kind of you not to pass by our door.

RANK: I thought I heard your voice, and felt as if I should like to look in. (*With a swift glance round.*) Ah, yes!—these dear familiar rooms. You are very happy and cosy in here, you two.

HELMER: It seems to me that you looked after yourself pretty well upstairs too.

RANK: Excellently. Why shouldn't I? Why shouldn't one enjoy everything in this world?—at any rate as much as one can, and as long as one can. The wine was capital—

HELMER: Especially the champagne.

RANK: So you noticed that too? It is almost incredible how much I managed to put away!

NORA: Torvald drank a great deal of champagne tonight too.

RANK: Did he?

NORA: Yes, and he is always in such good spirits afterwards.

RANK: Well, why should one not enjoy a merry evening after a well-spent day?

HELMER: Well spent? I am afraid I can't take credit for that.

RANK (*clapping him on the back*): But I can, you know!

NORA: Doctor Rank, you must have been occupied with some scientific investigation today.

RANK: Exactly.

HELMER: Just listen!—little Nora talking about scientific investigations!

NORA: And may I congratulate you on the result?

RANK: Indeed you may.

NORA: Was it favourable, then?

RANK: The best possible, for both doctor and patient—certainty.

NORA (*quickly and searchingly*): Certainty?

RANK: Absolute certainty. So wasn't I entitled to make a merry evening of it after that?

NORA: Yes, you certainly were, Doctor Rank.

HELMER: I think so too, so long as you don't have to pay for it in the morning.

RANK: Oh well, one can't have anything in this life without paying for it.

NORA: Doctor Rank—do you like fancy-dress balls?

RANK: Yes, if there is a fine lot of pretty costumes.

NORA: Tell me—what shall we two wear at the next?

HELMER: Little featherbrain!—are you thinking of the next already?

RANK: We two? Yes, I can tell you. You shall go as a good fairy—

HELMER: Yes, but what do you suggest as an appropriate costume for that?

RANK: Let your wife go dressed just as she is in everyday life.

HELMER: That was really very nicely said. But can't you tell us what you will be?

RANK: Yes, my dear friend, I have quite made up my mind about that.

HELMER: Well?

RANK: At the next fancy-dress ball I shall be invisible.

HELMER: That's a good joke?

RANK: There is a big black hat—have you never heard of hats that make you invisible? If you put one on, no one can see you.

HELMER (*suppressing a smile*): Yes, you are quite right.

RANK: But I am clean forgetting what I came for. Helmer, give me a cigar—one of the dark Havanas.

HELMER: With the greatest pleasure. (*Offers him his case.*)

RANK (*takes a cigar and cuts off the end*): Thanks.

NORA (*striking a match*): Let me give you a light.

RANK: Thank you. (*She holds the match for him to light his cigar.*) And now good-bye!

HELMER: Good-bye, good-bye, dear old man!

NORA: Sleep well, Doctor Rank.

RANK: Thank you for that wish.

NORA: Wish me the same.

RANK: You? Well, if you want me to sleep well! And thanks fcr the light. (*He nods to them both and goes out.*)

HELMER (*in a subdued voice*): He has drunk more than he ought.

NORA (*absently*): Maybe. (HELMER *takes a bunch of keys out of his pocket and goes into the hall.*) Torvald! what are you going to do there?

HELMER: Empty the letter box; it's quite full; there will be no room to put the newspaper in tomorrow morning.

NORA: Are you going to work tonight?

HELMER: You know quite well I'm not. What's this? Someone has been at the lock.

NORA: At the lock—?

HELMER: Yes, someone has. What can it mean? I should never have thought the maid—Here is a broken hairpin. Nora, it is one of yours.

NORA (*quickly*): Then it must have been the children—

HELMER: Then you must get them out of those ways. There, at last I have got it open. (*Takes out the contents of the letter-box, and calls to the kitchen.*) Helen!—Helen, put out the light over the front door. (*Goes back into the room and shuts the door into the hall. He holds out his hand full of letters.*) Look at that—look what a heap of them there are. (*Turning them over.*) What on earth is that?

NORA (*at the window*): The letter—No! Torvald, no!

HELMER: Two cards—of Rank's.

NORA: Of Doctor Rank's?

HELMER (*looking at them*): Doctor Rank. They were on the top. He must have put them in when he went out.

NORA: Is there anything written on them?

HELMER: There is a black cross over the name. Look there—what an uncomfortable idea! It looks as if he were announcing his own death.

NORA: It is just what he is doing.

HELMER: What? Do you know anything about it? Has he said anything to you?

NORA: Yes. He told me that when the cards came it would be his leave-taking from us. He means to shut himself up and die.

HELMER: My poor old friend! I knew of course we shouldn't have him very long with us. But so soon! And so he hides himself away like a wounded animal.

NORA: If it has to happen, it is best it should be without a word—don't you think so, Torvald?

HELMER (*walking up and down*): He had so grown into our lives. I can't think of him as having gone out of them. With his sufferings and his loneliness, he was like a cloudy background to our sunlit happiness. Well, perhaps it is best so. For him, anyway. (*Standing still.*) And perhaps for us too, Nora. We two are thrown quite upon each other now. (*Puts his arms round her.*) My darling wife, I don't feel as if I could hold you tight enough. Do you know, Nora, I have often wished that you might be threatened by some great danger, so that I might risk my life's blood, and everything, for your sake.

NORA (*disengages herself, and says firmly and decidedly*): Now you must read your letters, Torvald.

HELMER: No, no; not tonight. I want to be with you, my darling wife.

NORA: With the thought of your friend's death—

HELMER: You are right, it has affected us both. Something ugly has come between us—the thought of the horrors of death. We must try and rid our minds of that. Until then—we will each go to our own room.

NORA (*hanging on his neck*): Good night, Torvald—good night!

HELMER (*kissing her on the forehead*): Good night, my little singing-bird. Sleep well, Nora. Now I will read my letters through. (*He takes his letters and goes into his room, shutting the door after him.*)

NORA (*gropes distractedly about, seizes* HELMER'S *domino, throws it round her, while she says in quick, hoarse, spasmodic whispers*): Never to see him again. Never! Never! (*Puts her shawl over her head.*) Never to see my children again either—never again. Never! Never!—oh! the icy, black water—the bottomless depths—if only it were over! He has got it now—now he is reading it. Good-bye, Torvald and my children! (*She is about to rush out through the hall, when* HELMER *opens his door hurriedly and stands with an open letter in his hand.*)

HELMER: NORA!

NORA: Oh!—

HELMER: What is this? Do you know what is in this letter?

NORA: Yes, I know. Let me go! Let me get out!

HELMER (*holding her back*): Where are you going?

NORA (*trying to get free*): You shan't save me, Torvald!

HELMER (*reeling*): True? Is this true, that I read here? Horrible! No, no—it's impossible that it can be true.

NORA: It is true. I have loved you above everything else in the world.

HELMER: Oh, don't let us have any silly excuses.

NORA (*taking a step towards him*): Torvald—!

HELMER: Miserable creature—what have you done?

NORA: Let me go. You shall not suffer for my sake. You shall not take it upon yourself.

HELMER: No tragedy airs, please. (*Locks the hall door.*) Here you shall stay and give me an explanation. Do yon understand what you have done? Answer me! Do you understand what you have done?

NORA (*looks steadily at him and says with a growing look of coldness in her face*): Yes, now I am beginning to understand thoroughly.

HELMER (*walking about the room*): What a horrible awakening! All these eight years—she who was my pride and joy—a hypocrite, a liar—worse, worse—a criminal! The unutterable ugliness of it all!—What disgraceful behaviour! (NORA *is silent and looks steadily at him. He stops in front of her.*) I ought to have foreseen it. All your father's want of principle—be silent!—all your father's want of principle has come out in you. No religion, no morality, no sense of duty—How I am punished for having winked at what he did! I did it for your sake, and this is how you repay me.

NORA: Yes, that's just it.

HELMER: Now you have destroyed all my happiness. You have ruined all my future. It is horrible to think of! I am in the power of an unscrupulous man; he can do what he likes with me, ask anything he likes of me, give me any orders he pleases—I dare not refuse. And I must sink to such miserable depths because of a thoughtless woman!

NORA: When I am out of the way, you will be free.

HELMER: No fine speeches, please. Your father had always plenty of those ready, too. What good would it be to me if you were out of the way, as you say? Not the slightest. He can make the affair known everywhere; and if he does, I may be falsely suspected of having been a party to your criminal action. Very likely people will think I was behind it alt—that it was I who prompted you! And I have to thank you for all this—you whom I have cherished during the whole of our married life. Do you understand now what it is you have done for me?

NORA (*coldly and quietly*): Yes.

HELMER: It is so incredible that I can't take it in. But we must come to some understanding. Take off that shawl. Take it off, I tell you. I must try and appease him some way or another. The matter must be hushed up at any cost. And as for you and me, it must appear as if everything between us were just as before—but naturally only in the eyes of the world. You will still remain in my house, that is a matter of course. But I shall not allow you to bring up the children; I dare not trust them to you. To think that I should have to say this to one whom I have loved so dearly, and whom I still—No, that is all over. From this moment happiness is not the question; all that concerns us is to save the remains, the fragments, the appearance—(*A ring is heard at the front-door bell.*)

HELMER (*witk a start*): What is that? So late! Can the worst—? Can he—? Hide yourself, Nora. Say you are ill.

(NORA *stands motionless,* HELMER *goes and unlocks the hall door.*)

MAID (*half-dressed, comes to the door*): A letter for the mistress.

HELMER: Give it to me. (*Takes the letter, and shuts the door.*) Yes. it is from him. You shall not have it; I will read it myself.

NORA: Yes, read it.

HELMER (*standing by the lamp*): I scarcely have the courage to do it. It may mean ruin for both of us. No, I must know. (*Tears open the letter, runs his eye over a few lines, looks at a paper enclosed, and gives a shout of joy.*) Nora! (*She looks at him questioningly.*) Nora!—No I must read it once again—Yes, it is true! I am saved! Nora, I am saved!

NORA: And I?

HELMER: You too, of course; we are both saved, both you and I. Look, he sends you your bond back. He says he regrets and repents—that a happy change in his life—never mind what he says! We are saved, Nora! No one can do anything to you. Oh, Nora, Nora!—no, first I must destroy these hateful things. Let me see—(*Takes a look at the bond.*) No, no, I won't look at it. The whole thing shall be nothing but a bad dream to me. (*Tears up the bond and both letters, throws them all into the stove, and watches them burn.*) There—now it doesn't exist any longer. He says that since Christmas Eve you—These must have been three dreadful days for you, Nora.

NORA: I have fought a hard fight these three days.

HELMER: And suffered agonies, and seen no way out but—No, we won't call any of the horrors to mind. We will only shout with joy, and keep saying, 'It's all over! It's all over!' Listen to me, Nora. You don't seem to realize that it is all over. What is this?—such a cold, set face! My poor little Nora, I quite understand; you don't feel as if you could believe that I have forgiven you. But it is true, Nora, I swear it; I have forgiven you everything. I know that what you did, you did out of love for me.

NORA: That is true.

HELMER: You have loved me as a wife ought to love her husband. Only you had not sufficient knowledge to judge of the means you used. But do you suppose you are any the less dear to me, because you don't understand how to act on your own responsibility? No, no; just lean on me; I will advise you and direct you. I shouldn't be a man if this womanly helplessness did not actually give you a double attractiveness in my eyes. You mustn't think any more about the hard things I said in my first moment of consternation, when I thought everything was going to overwhelm me. I have forgiven you, Nora; I swear to you I have forgiven you.

NORA: Thank you for your forgiveness. (*She goes out through the door to the right.*)

HELMER: No, don't go—(*Looks in.*) What are you doing in there?

NORA (*from within*): Taking off my fancy dress.

HELMER (*standing at the open door*): Yes, do. Try and calm yourself, and make your mind easy again, my frightened little singing-bird. Relax, and feel secure; I have broad wings to shelter you under. (*Walks up and down by the door.*) How warm and cosy our home is, Nora. Here is shelter for you; here I will protect you like a hunted dove that I have saved from a hawk's claws; I will bring peace to your poor beating heart. It will come, little by little, Nora, believe me. Tomorrow morning you will look upon it all quite differently; soon everything will be just as it was before. Very soon you won't need me to assure you that I have forgiven you; you will yourself feel the certainty that I have done so. Do you imagine I should ever think of such a thing as repudiating you, or even reproaching you? You have no idea what a true man's heart is like, Nora. There is something so indescribably sweet and satisfying, to a man, in the knowledge that he has forgiven his wife—forgiven her freely, and with all his heart. It seems as if that had made her, as it were, doubly his own; he has given her a new life, so to speak; and she has in a way become both wife and child to him. So you shall be for me after this, my little scared, helpless darling. Have no anxiety about anything, Nora; just be frank and open with me, and I will serve as will and conscience both to you—What is this? Not gone to bed? Have you changed your things?

NORA (*in everyday dress*): Yes, Torvald, I have changed my things now.

HELMER: But what for?—as late as this.

NORA: I shan't sleep tonight.

HELMER: But, my dear Nora—

NORA (*looking at her watch*): It is not so very late. Sit down here, Torvald. You and I have a lot to say to one another. (*She sits down at one side of the table.*)

HELMER: Nora—what is this?—this cold, set face?

NORA: Sit down. It will take some time; I have a lot to talk over with you.

HELMER (*sits down at the opposite side of the table*): You alarm me, Nora!—and I don't understand you.

NORA: No, that is just it. You don't understand me, and I have never understood you either—before tonight. No, you mustn't interrupt me. You must simply listen to what I say. Torvald, this is a settling of accounts.

HELMER: What do you mean by that?

NORA (*after a short silence*): Isn't there one thing that strikes you as strange in our sitting here like this?

HELMER: What is that?

NORA: We have been married now eight years. Doesn't it occur to you that this is the first time we two, you and I, husband and wife, have had a serious conversation?

HELMER: What do you mean by serious?

NORA: In all these eight years—longer than that—from the very beginning of our acquaintance, we have never exchanged a word on any serious subject.

HELMER: Was it likely that I would be continually and for ever telling you about worries that you could not help me to bear?

NORA: I am not speaking about business matters. I say that we have never sat down in earnest together to try and get at the bottom of anything.

HELMER: But, dearest Nora, would it have been any good to you?

NORA: That is just it; you have never understood me. I have been greatly wronged, Torvald—first by father and then by you.

HELMER: What! By us two—by us two, who have loved you better than anyone else in the world?

NORA (*shaking her head*): You have never loved me. You have only thought it pleasant to be in love with me.

HELMER: Nora, what do I hear you saying?

NORA: It is perfectly true, Torvald. When I was at home with father, he told me his opinion about everything, and so I had the same opinions; and if I differed from him I concealed the fact, because he would not have liked it. He called me his doll-child, and he played with me just as I used to play with my dolls. And when I came to live with you—

HELMER: What sort of an expression is that to use about our marriage!

NORA (*undisturbed*): I mean that I was simply transferred from father's hands into yours. You arranged everything according to your own taste, and so I got the same tastes as you—or else I pretended to, I am really not quite sure which—I think sometimes the one and sometimes the other. When I look back on it, it seems to me as if I had been living here like a poor woman—just from hand to mouth. I have existed merely to perform tricks for you, Torvald. But you wanted it like that. You and father have committed a great sin against me. It is your fault that I have made nothing of my life.

HELMER: How unreasonable and how ungrateful you are, Nora! Haven't you been happy here?

NORA: No, I have never been happy. I thought I was, but it has never really been so.

HELMER: Not—not happy!

NORA: No, only merry. And you have always been so kind to me. But our home has been nothing but a playroom. I have been your doll-wife, just as at home I was father's doll-child; and here the children have been my dolls. I thought it great fun when you played with me, just as they thought it great fun when I played with them. That is what our marriage has been, Torvald.

HELMER: There is some truth in what you say—exaggerated and strained as your view of it is. But in future it will be different. Playtime is over, and lesson-time will begin.

NORA: Whose lessons? Mine, or the children's?

HELMER: Both yours and the children's, my darling Nora.

NORA: I'm afraid, Torvald, you are not the man to educate me into being a proper wife for you.

HELMER: And you can say that!

NORA: And I—how am I fitted to bring up the children?

HELMER: Nora!

NORA: Didn't you say so yourself a little while ago—that you dare not trust me to bring them up?

HELMER: In a moment of anger! Why do you take any notice of that?

NORA: Actually, you were perfectly right. I am not fit for the task. There is another task I must undertake first. I must try and educate myself—you are not the man to help me in that. I must do that for myself. And that is why I am going to leave you now.

HELMER (*springing up*): What are you saying?

NORA: I must stand quite alone, if I am to understand myself and everything about me. It is for that reason that I cannot remain with you any longer.

HELMER: Nora, Nora!

NORA: I am going away from here now, at once. I am sure Christine will take me in for the night—

HELMER: You are out of your mind! I won't allow it! I forbid you!

NORA: It is no use forbidding me anything any longer. I will take with me only what belongs to me. I will take nothing from you, either now or later.

HELMER: What sort of madness is this!

NORA: Tomorrow I shall go home—I mean, to my old home. It will be easiest for me to find something to do there.

HELMER: You blind, foolish woman!

NORA: I must try and get some sense, Torvald.

HELMER: To desert your home, your husband, and your children! And you don't consider what people will say!

NORA: I cannot consider that at all. I only know that it is necessary for me.

HELMER: It's shocking. This is how you would neglect your most sacred duties.

NORA: What do you consider my most sacred duties?

HELMER: Do I need to tell you that? Are they not your duties to your husband and your children?

NORA: I have other duties just as sacred.

HELMER: Indeed you have not. What duties could those be?

NORA: Duties to myself.

HELMER: Before all else, you are a wife and a mother.

NORA: I don't believe that any longer. I believe that before all else I am a reasonable human being, just as you are—or, at all events, that I must try and become one. I know quite well, Torvald, that most people would think you right, and that views of that kind are to be found in books; but I can no longer content myself with what most people say, or with what is found in books. I must think over things for myself and get to understand them.

HELMER: Can you not understand your place in your own home? Have you not a reliable guide in such matters as that?—have you no religion?

NORA: I am afraid, Torvald, I do not exactly know what religion is.

HELMER: What are you saying?

NORA: I know nothing but what the clergyman said, when I went to be confirmed. He told us that religion was this, and that, and the other. When I am away from all this and am alone, I will look into that matter too. I will see if what the clergyman said is true, or at all events if it is true for me.

HELMER: This is unheard of in a girl of your age! But if religion cannot lead you aright, let me try and awaken your conscience. I suppose you have some moral sense? Or—answer me—am I to think you have none?

NORA: I assure you, Torvald, that is not an easy question to answer. I really don't know. The thing perplexes me altogether. I only know that you and I look at it in quite a different light. I am learning, too, that the law is quite another thing from what I supposed; but I find it impossible to convince myself that the law is right. According to it a woman has no right to spare her old dying father, or to save her husband's life. I can't believe that.

HELMER: You talk like a child. You don't understand the conditions of the world in which you live.

NORA: No, I don't. But now I am going to try. I am going to see if I can make out who is right, the world or I.

HELMER: You are ill, Nora; you are delirious; I almost think you are out of your mind.

NORA: I have never felt my mind so clear and certain as tonight.

HELMER: And is it with a clear and certain mind that you forsake your husband and your children?

NORA: Yes, it is.

HELMER: Then there is only one possible explanation.

NORA: What is that?

HELMER: You do not love me any more.

NORA: No, that is just it.

HELMER: Nora!—and you can say that?

NORA: It gives me great pain, Torvald, because you have always been so kind to me, but I cannot help it. I don't love you any more.

HELMER (*regaining his composure*): Is that a clear and certain conviction too?

NORA: Yes, absolutely clear and certain. That is the reason why I will not stay here any longer.

HELMER: And can you tell me what I have done to forfeit your love?

NORA: Yes, indeed I can. It was tonight, when the wonderful thing did not happen; then I saw you were not the man I had thought you.

HELMER: Explain yourself better. I don't understand you.

NORA: I have waited so patiently for eight years; for, goodness knows, I knew very well that wonderful things don't happen every day. Then this horrible misfortune came upon me; and then I felt quite certain that the wonderful thing was going to happen at last. When Krogstad's letter was lying out there, never for a moment did I imagine that you would consent to accept this man's conditions. I was so absolutely certain that you would say to him: Publish the thing to the whole world. And when that was done—

HELMER: Yes, what then?—when I had exposed my wife to shame and disgrace?

NORA: When that was done, I was so absolutely certain, you would come forward and take everything upon yourself, and say: I am the guilty one.

HELMER: Nora—!

NORA: You mean that I would never have accepted such a sacrifice on your part? No, of course not. But what would my assurances have been worth against yours? That was the wonderful thing which I hoped for and feared; and it was to prevent that, that I wanted to kill myself.

HELMER: I would gladly work night and day for you, Nora—bear sorrow and want for your sake. But no man would sacrifice his honour for the one he loves.

NORA: It is a thing hundreds of thousands of women have done.

HELMER: Oh, you think and talk like a thoughtless child.

NORA: May be. But you neither think nor talk like the man I could bind myself to. As soon as your fear was over—and it was not fear for what threatened me, but for what might happen to you—when the whole thing was past, as far as you were concerned it was exactly as if nothing at all had happened. Exactly as before, I was your little skylark, your doll, which you would in future treat with doubly gentle care, because it was so brittle and fragile. (*Getting up.*) Torvald—it was then it dawned upon me that for eight years I had been living here with a strange man, and had borne him three children—Oh, I can't bear to think of it! I could tear myself into little bits!

HELMER (*sadly*): I see, I see. An abyss has opened between us—there is no denying it. But, Nora, would it not be possible to fill it up?

NORA: As I am now, I am no wife for you.

HELMER: I have it in me to become a different man.

NORA: Perhaps—if your doll is taken away from you.

HELMER: But to part!—to part from you! No, no, Nora, I can't understand that idea.

NORA (*going out to the right*): That makes it all the more certain that it must be done. (*She comes back with her cloak and hat and a small bag which she puts on a chair by the table.*)

HELMER: Nora, Nora, not now! Wait till tomorrow.

NORA (*putting on her cloak*): I cannot spend the night in a strange man's room.

HELMER: But can't we live here like brother and sister—?

NORA (*putting on her hat*): You know very well that wouldn't last long. (*Puts the shawl round her.*) Good-bye, Torvald. I won't see the little ones. I know they are in better hands than mine. As I am now, I can be of no use to them.

HELMER: But some day, Nora—some day?

NORA: How can I tell? I have no idea what is going to become of me.

HELMER: But you are my wife, whatever becomes of you.

NORA: Listen, Torvald. I have heard that when a wife deserts her husband's house, as I am doing now, he is legally freed from all obligations towards her. In any case I set you free from all obligations. You are not to feel yourself bound in the slightest way, any more than I shall. There must be perfect freedom on both sides. See, here is your ring back. Give me mine.

HELMER: That too?

NORA: That too.

HELMER: Here it is.

NORA: That's right. Now it is all over. I have put the keys here. The maids know all about everything in the house—better than I do. Tomorrow, after I have left her, Christine will come here and pack up my own things that I brought with me from home. I will have them sent after me.

HELMER: All over! All over!—Nora, will you never think of me again?

NORA: I know I shall often think of you and the children and this house.

HELMER: May I write to you, Nora?

NORA: No—Never. You must not do that.

HELMER: But at least let me send you—

NORA: Nothing—nothing—

HELMER: Let me help you if you are in want.

NORA: No. I can receive nothing from a stranger.

HELMER: Nora—can I never be anything more than a stranger to you?

NORA (*taking her bag*): Ah, Torvald, the most wonderful thing of all would have to happen.

HELMER: Tell me what that would be!

NORA: Both you and I would have to be so changed that—Oh, Torvald, I don't believe any longer in wonderful things happening.

HELMER: But I will believe in it. Tell me! So changed that—?

NORA: That our life together would be a real marriage. Good-bye. (*She goes out through the hall.*)

HELMER (*sinks down on a chair at the door and buries his face in his hands*): Nora! Nora! (*Looks round, and rises.*) Empty. She is gone. (*A hope flashes across his mind.*) The most wonderful thing of all—?

(*The sound of a door shutting is heard from below.*)

****

NOTES

ACT I

footlights: a row of lights along the front edge of the floor of a stage at the theatre.

rocking-chair: a chair that swings to and fro when pushed.

china: crockery.

outdoor dress: dress worn outside the house.

Porter: a person who carries loads for hire.

Christmas-tree: a real or man-made tree ornamented at Christmas with candles, lights, coloured paper, etc., often brought into the home. Commenting on its significance John Northam (*Ibsen's Dramatic Method,* p.19) says: 'Christmas is a family festival, mainly devoted to the happiness of children, and the tree is its symbol, epitomizing family happiness and security. We see the tree just long enough for it to suggest ideas of this kind, and then the maid takes it away'.

Torvald: Peter Watts (*A Doll's House and Other Plays,* Penguin Books, p. 333) says: 'Almost alone among Ibsen's married women, Nora always calls her husband by his Christian name. It would have been more usual to call him simply "Helmer".'

wee bit: a little.

featherbrain: a frivolous person.

my little...wings: need not be depressed. Mark how Helmer addresses his wife.

wheedling: coaxing.

wagging: moving.

Miss Sweet-Tooth: one who is fond of sweet and sugary things.

macaroon: small sweet cake or biscuit made of sugar, white of egg and crushed almonds.

nibbling: eating with small bites.

unsavoury: unacceptable in moral values.

odds and ends: small articles of various kinds.

crochet-work: fancy-work done with a needle which has a small hook at one end.

precarious: uncertain.

fend for: provide for.

backwater: a place or condition of mind untouched by events, progress, etc.

broach: introduce.

palled: became uninteresting or dull.

scrape together: save with difficulty.

romp: play noisily and roughly with a lot of running and jumping.

makes up fire in the stove: 'There is no real need for Nora to touch the stove, but the action illuminates the whole passage. The stage directions and the dialogue tell us that Nora fears Krogstad; the action thrusts home the impression; he has chilled her with terror, so she makes up the fire, instinctively seeking a physical remedy for a nervous discomfort' (John Northam, p. 18).

snuffing: sniffing.

lucrative: profitable.

healthy natures: honest men.

shrugging his shoulders: expressive of doubt, indifference, or disdain.

sick-house: hospital.

smothered: suppressed.

draught: current of air in a room or any shut-in place.

ajar: partly open.

construction: meaning or sense given to a statement.

slightingly: disrespectfully.

indiscretion: an unwise act.

blackguard: scoundrel.

amiss: wrong.

Here.. .floor: 'the tree is set in the middle of the floor, where, for the audience, it becomes the chief point of interest, dominating the stage with suggestions of family security and happiness; in it, and in Nora's "dressing", we see her desire to reassert her family's threatened safety and to reassure herself in her sharp uneasiness' (John Northam, p. 20).

snug: cosy, warm and comfortable.

gone under: morally ruined.

dissimulation: false pretension; hypocrisy.

gold paper: gilt paper.

ACT II

The Christmas-tree...branches: 'The symbol of family security no longer holds the centre, nor is it in its full Christmas glory. It is stripped and it stands in a corner, just as Nora has been chastened and frightened by the intrusion of the unfeeling masculine world of business' (John Northam, p. 21).

stripped: 'In Scandinavia the Christmas tree and its presents are enjoyed on Christmas Eve' (Peter Watts, p. 333).

dishevelled: in disarray.

confirmed: admitted to the full membership of the church.

muff: covering, usually a cylindrical padded bag of fur, used by a woman to keep the hands warm.

Out of...thoughts: Let me not think about it.

One...six: She resorts to counting just to divert her mind.

irresolute: undecided.

Neapolitan: belonging to Naples.

Tarantella: a lively Neapolitan dance in triplets for one couple.

Capri: an island in West Italy in the Bay of Naples.

keep up the character: to give a real performance.

prevaricate: try to evade telling the (whole) truth.

scurrilous: vulger; using violent and taunting words of abuse.

interceding: pleading.

pen-pusher: clerk.

tambourine: a shallow single-headed drum with jingles, played on with the hand.

It is all up with me: I am at my end; likely to die.

dissolution: death.

loathsome: disgusting.

inexorable: unrelenting.

retribution: requital: deserved punishment.

asparagus: a plant whose young green stems are eaten as a vegetable.

pâtè de foie gras: pâtè (patty) made from the liver of a goose.

truffles: a type of fleshy blackish or light brown fungus that grows underground and is highly regarded as a food.

oyester: a kind of shell-fish much used as food, usually eated uncooked.

port: strong (usually sweet) dark-red Portuguese wine, usually drunk after a meal.

champagne: a type of costly French white wine containing a lot of bubbles, usually drunk on special occasions.

restricted: narrow.

Krogstad's footsteps are heard: 'One of the rare occasions where Ibsen's practical stagecraft deserts him. If he had remembered his days as stage manager at Bergen, he would have realized how heavy-footed Krogstad would have to be if the audience were to hear him. In Act Three Ibsen even specifics that they are "soft foot-steps" (Peter Watts, p. 334).

out of your mind: mad.

Nora, at the...Tarantella: 'We have grown more aware of the increasing torment in her soul, but the drama demands that, at its height, the agony should be concealed from the others in the play—but not from us, or the pathos and irony would be lost. And so Nora's frantic struggle against fate is represented in action, in the tarantella, traditionally the dance of victims of the poisonous spider' (John Northam, p. 18).

bars: a few notes of music considered to form a group.

variegated shawl: symbolic of 'the persistence of a desire to maintain her old form of happiness' (John Northam, p. 23).

the small hours: the three or four hours after midnight.

ACT III

Nils: Krogstad's Christian name, used to suggest intimacy.

jilts: discards (a lover) after giving encouragement or promise to marry.

shipwrecked: ruined.

wreckage: the broken parts of a destroyed thing.

black shawl: symbolic of her death-wish.

domino: loose cloak with a mask for the upper part of the face, worn at parties, fancy-dress balls, etc.

capricious: whimsical.

curtsy: curtesy.

apparition: phantom.

Pooh!: an expression of impatience.

Chinese effect: grotesque.

seductive: alluring.

figures: set of movements in a dance.

on fire: burning.

put away: drink.

balls: social gatherings for dancing, with an organised programme and special entertainment.

Havanas: a fine quality of cigar, fondly supposed to be made at Havana (Cuba).

distractedly: confused or bewildered.

spasmodic: taking place at irregular intervals.

winked at: deliberately ignored.

consternation: dismay.

repudiating: disowning.

delirious: wildly excited.

forfeit: have to suffer the loss, as a punishment or consequence.

the wonderful thing: Nora had believed that Helmer would take on him the responsibility of her crime.

brittle: frail.

fragile: delicate.

****

QUESTIONS

(a) *On Ibsen*

1. What is Ibsen's distinctive contribution to the history of drama?
2. 'With Ibsen the history of drama begins anew' (George Steiner). Comment.
3. How far is it correct to call Ibsen the 'Father of the modern drama'?
4. 'Ibsen, as a dramatist, is neither primarily a thinker nor a psychologist; he is an illusionist and artist' (P.F.D. Tennant). Do you agree with this view?
5. 'Ibsen was a realist outside, a fantasist inside' (Eric Bentley). Discuss.
6. 'We live in, not look at, a play by Ibsen' (R. E. Roberts). Explain.
7. Do you agree with the view that Ibsen's last plays mark a decline in his dramatic power?
8. What is a 'well-made' play? Trace its influence on Ibsen's dramatic art.
9. 'Ibsen took the conventions of the day and adapted them for his own ends' (M. C. Bradbrook). Amplify and illustrate.
10. In what ways Ibsen's social plays differ from the contemporary social drama?
11. What do you understand by 'the drama of ideas'? Can we place Ibsen's social dramas under this category?
12. What is the 'retrospective method'? How does Ibsen use it in his plays? What purpose does it serve?

(b) *On 'A Doll's House'*

1. Give an account of the contemporary reception of *A Doll's House*. What was it that made it so remarkable?
2. '*A Doll's House* fell like a bomb into contemporary life' (H. Koht). Explain.
3. '*A Doll's House* stands in relation to modern drama as Queen Victoria to the royal families of Europe' (M. C. Bradbrook). Expand.
4. Do you find in *A Doll's House* any evidence of 'Ibsen's capacity for Conveying unspoken thought'? If so, give some examples.
5. Comment on the theme of *A Doll's House.*
6. M. C. Bradbrook observes that *A Doll's House* 'offers a particular artist's vision which is inseparable from the manner of its formulation'. Discuss the play in the light of the above remark.
7. How does the dialogue between Nora and Mrs Linde in the first act advance the story?
8. What is the purpose of the scene between Nora, Dr Rank and Mrs Linde in Act I ?
9. Do you see any reason why Helmer should speak of Krogstad in the first act rather than in a later one?
10. What dramatic purpose is served by the conversation between Nora and the Nurse at the opening of Act II?
11. Nora's saying that 'worse than that might happen' (II, 25) is a good instance of 'foreshadowing'. Can you quote some other examples from the play?
12. What structural purpose is served by Dr Rank's exposition of his views on heredity?
13. How far s Dr Rank relevant to the central theme of the play? Can we not do without him?
14. Do you agree with the view that Nora 'lacks dramatic consistency' (Storm Jameson)? Give your reasons.
15. Why does Ibsen contrive a rather long scene between Nora and Dr Rank in Act II? Does it serve any essential dramatic purpose ?
16. Some critics think that Nora's conversion from a 'doll' into a mature thinking woman in Act III is 'too sudden to be dramatically credible'. Do you agree with this opinion?

17. How does Ibsen prepare the ground for the final scene between Helmer and Nora?
18. Of Helmer R. E. Roberts says: 'the man is, in a crisis, a cad'. Do you agree with this view?
19. Comment on the dramatic significance of the following: the Christmas-tree, the macaroons, and tarantella.
20. What traces of the 'well-made' drama do you find in *A Doll's House?* Wherein does it depart from that?

****

Select Bibliography

Bentley, Eric, *The Playwright as Thinker*, Meridian Books, Cleveland & New York: The World Publishing Company, 1964.

Beyer, Edvard, *Ibsen: The Man and His Work*, London, Souvenir Press, 1978. (This contains a comprehensive bibliography.)

Bradbrook, M. C, *Ibsen the Norwegian: A Revaluation*, London: Chat to & Windus, 1946.

Cole, Toby (ed.), *Playwrights on Playwriting*, New York: Hill & Wang, 1964.

Downs, Brian W., *Ibsen: The Intellectual Background*, Cambridge: The University Press, 1946.

—, *A Study of Six Plays by Ibsen*, Cambridge: The University Press, 1950. (The six plays are: *Love's Comedy, Brand, Peer Gynt, A Doll's House, The Wild Duck*, and *The Master Builder*.)

Egan, Michael (ed.), *Ibsen: The Critical Heritage*, London: Routledge & Kegan Paul Ltd., 1972.

Fjelde, R. (ed.), *Ibsen: A Collection of Critical Essays*, The Twentieth-Century Views Series, Englewood Cliffs, N. J.: Prentice-Hall, 1966.

Gassner, John, *Masters of the Drama*, Third Revised and Enlarged Edition, Dover Publications.

—(ed.), *Ideas in the Drama*, New York & London: Columbia University Press, 1964.

Granville-Barker, H., *On Dramatic Method*, New York: Hill & Wang, 1964. Jameson, Storm, *Modern Drama in Europe*, London: W. Collins Sons & Co., 1920.

Koht, H., *The Life of Ibsen*, 2 vols., London: George Allen & Unwin, 1931. Krutch, Joseph Wood, *'Modernism' in Modern Drama*, New York: Cornell University Press, 1953.

Lamm, Martin, *Modern Drama*, translated by Karin Elliott, Oxford: Basil Blackwell, 1952.

Lavrin, Janko, *Ibsen: An Approach*, London: Methuen & Co., 1950.

McFarlane, J. W., *Ibsen and the Temper of Norwegian Literature*, London: Oxford University Press, 1960.

Nicoll, A., *World Drama*, London: George G. Harrap & Co., 1964.

Northam, John, *Ibsen's Dramatic Method*, London: Faber & Faber, 1953.

Roberts, R., Ellis, *Henrik Ibsen: A Critical Study*, London: Martin Secker, 1912.

Shaw, G. B., *Major Critical Essays*, London: Constable & Company, 1932.

(Contains the expanded edition of *The Quintessence of Ibsenism).*

—, *Dramatic Opinions and Essays*. 3 vols, New York: Brentano's, 1928.

Tennant, P. F. D., *Ibsen's Dramatic Technique*, Cambridge: Bowes & Bowes, 1948.

Williams, Raymond, *Drama from Ibsen to Eliot*, Penguin Books, 1964.

****